HABEAS CORPUS

by the same author

FORTY YEARS ON
GETTING ON

Habeas Corpus

A Play in Two Acts
by
ALAN BENNETT

FABER AND FABER
3 Queen Square
London

First published in 1973
by Faber and Faber Limited
3 Queen Square London WC1
Reprinted 1975
Printed in Great Britain by
Whitstable Litho Ltd Whitstable Kent
All rights reserved

ISBN 0 571 10509 2 (paper covers)

Characters

ARTHUR WICKSTEED, a General Practitioner
MURIEL WICKSTEED, his wife
DENNIS WICKSTEED, their son
CONSTANCE WICKSTEED, the doctor's sister
MRS. SWABB, a cleaning lady
CANON THROBBING, a celibate
LADY RUMPERS, a white settler
FELICITY RUMPERS, her daughter
MR. SHANKS, a sales representative
SIR PERCY SHORTER, a leading light in the medical profession
MR. PURDUE, a sick man

All scenes take place in and around the
Wicksteeds' house in Hove.

When the play opened at the Lyric Theatre on 10th May 1973 the cast was as follows:

ARTHUR WICKSTEED	Alec Guinness
MURIEL WICKSTEED	Margaret Courtenay
DENNIS WICKSTEED	Christopher Good
CONSTANCE WICKSTEED	Phyllida Law
MRS. SWABB	Patricia Hayes
CANON THROBBING	Roddy Maude-Roxby
LADY RUMPERS	Joan Sanderson
FELICITY RUMPERS	Madeline Smith
MR. SHANKS	Andrew Sachs
SIR PERCY SHORTER	John Bird
MR. PURDUE	Mike Carnell

Directed by Ronald Eyre
Designed by Derek Cousins
Music by Carl Davis

Presented by Michael Codron in association
with Stoll Productions

Author's Note

The text printed here is as first performed at the Lyric Theatre, London, in May 1973. In the rehearsal version of the play I included no stage directions in an effort to achieve as fluid a presentation as possible. In the printed version I have marked a minimum of entrances and exits to make the action more readily comprehensible to the reader.

The play was presented on an open stage furnished with three chairs. All props, telephone, parcel, etc., were handed in from the wings. Much of the dialogue was delivered straight to the audience to an extent that makes it tedious to indicate all remarks taken as asides.

I would like to thank Ronald Eyre for his invaluable assistance with the text.

ACT ONE

WICKSTEED: Look at him. Just look at that look on his face.
Do you know what that means? He wants me to tell him
he's not going to die. You're not going to die. He is going
to die. Not now, of course, but some time . . . ten, fifteen
years, who knows? I don't. We don't want to lose you, do
we? And off he goes. Sentence suspended. Another ten years.
Another ten years showing the slides. ("That's Malcolm,
Pauline and Baby Jason.") Another ten years going for little
runs in the car. ("That's us at the Safari Park.") "So what did
the doctor say, dear?" "Nothing, oh, nothing. It was all
imagination." But it's not all imagination. Sometimes I'm
afraid, it actually happens.
MRS. WICKSTEED'S VOICE: Arthur! Arthur!
MRS. SWABB: It's all in the mind. Me, I've never had a day's
illness in my life. No. I tell a lie. I once had my tonsils out.
I went in on the Monday; I had it done on the Tuesday;
I was putting wallpaper up on the Wednesday. My name is
Mrs. Swabb (hoover, hoover, hoover) someone who comes
in; and in all that passes, I represent ye working classes.
Hoover, hoover, hoover. Hoover, hoover, hoover. Now then,
let's have a little more light on the proceedings and meet
our contestants, the wonderful, wonderful Wicksteed family.
Eyes down first for tonight's hero, Dr. Arthur Wicksteed,
a general practitioner in Brighton's plush, silk stocking
district of Hove. Is that right, Doctor?
WICKSTEED: Hove, that's right, yes.
MRS. SWABB: And you are fifty-three years of age.
WICKSTEED: Dear God, am I?
MRS. SWABB: I'm afraid that's what I've got down here.

WICKSTEED: Fifty-three!

MRS. SWABB: Any hobbies?

WICKSTEED: No. No. Our friends, the ladies, of course, but nothing much else.

MRS. SWABB: Do you mind telling us what your ambition is?

WICKSTEED: Ambition? No, never had any. Partly the trouble, you see. When you've gone through life stopping at every lamp-post, no time.

MRS. SWABB: Next we have . . .

MRS. WICKSTEED: I can manage thank you. Elocution was always my strong point. Speak clearly, speak firmly, speak now. Name: Wicksteed, Muriel Jane. Age? Well, if you said fifty you'd be in the target area. Wife to the said Arthur Wicksteed and golly, don't I know it. Still potty about him though, the dirty dog. Oh, shut up, Muriel.

MRS. SWABB: And now . . . this is Dennis, only son of Arthur and Muriel Wicksteed. And what do you do, Dennis?

DENNIS: Nothing very much. I think I've got lockjaw.

MRS. SWABB: Really? Whereabouts?

DENNIS: All over.

MRS. SWABB: Are you interested in girls at all?

DENNIS: If they're clean.

MRS. SWABB: That goes without saying. You don't want a dirty girl, do you?

DENNIS: In a way, I do, yes.

MRS. WICKSTEED: Dennis!

MRS. SWABB: And now we have the doctor's sister, Miss Constance Wicksteed. Connie is a thirty-three-year-old spinster . . .

CONNIE: I am not a spinster. I am unmarried.

MRS. SWABB: And to go with her mud-coloured cardigan Connie has chosen a fetching number in form-fitting cretonne. Have you any boy friends, dear?

CONNIE: No.

MRS. SWABB: Connie, you big story! What about Canon Throbbing, our thrusting young vicar? Why! That sounds like his Biretta now.

(THROBBING *crosses the stage on his power-assisted bicycle*.)

12

Now, Connie, would you like to tell the audience what your ambition is? Go on, just whisper.

CONNIE: I'd like a big bust.

MRS. SWABB: And what would you do with it when you'd got it?

CONNIE: Flaunt it.

MRS. WICKSTEED: Connie!

MRS. SWABB: Three strangers too are in the town. A lady and her daughter. . . .

SIR PERCY: Out of my way, we're wasting time: I am Sir Percy Shorter. Shorter, Percy, K.C.B., President, British Medical Association. Venuing this week at Brighton.

MRS. WICKSTEED: Percy!

WICKSTEED: My wife's sometime sweetheart.

MRS. WICKSTEED: The man I spurned.

SIR PERCY: Well? Aren't you going to ask me what my ambition is?

MRS. SWABB: President of the British Medical Association! What more can a man want?

SIR PERCY: Revenge.

MRS. SWABB: I don't like it. Two strangers now are in the town, a lady and her daughter. . . .

LADY RUMPERS: England, my poor England. What have they done to you? Don't touch me. That's one thing I've noticed returning to these shores. There's a great deal more touching going on. If I want to be touched I have people who love me who can touch me. Touching is what loved ones are for, because loving takes the sting out of it. Delia, Lady Rumpers, widow of General Sir Frederick Rumpers. Tiger to his friends and to his enemies too, by God. Does the name Rumpers ring a bell?

WICKSTEED: Very, very faintly.

LADY RUMPERS: Time was when it would have rung all the bells in England. Rumpers of Rhodesia, Rumpers of Rangoon— when the history of the decline of the British Empire comes to be written, the name Rumpers will be in the index. For many years we were stationed in Addis Ababa. Tiger was right hand man to the Lion of Judah.

MRS. SWABB: Haile Selassie.

13

LADY RUMPERS: There followed a short spell in K.L.

MRS. SWABB: Kings Langley.

LADY RUMPERS: Kuala Lumpur.

MRS. WICKSTEED: Of course.

LADY RUMPERS: Then we fetched up in Rhodesia. In a green
    meadow on the outskirts of Salisbury, roses bloom and the
    trees are alive with the songs of multi-coloured birds. There
    we laid him.

    (DENNIS *sniffs*.)

    I am upsetting you?

CONNIE: He has hay fever.

LADY RUMPERS: From end to end I've searched the land looking
    for a place where England is still England.

WICKSTEED: And now she's hit on Hove.

LADY RUMPERS: My daughter. . . .

    (*Everyone looks but no one enters.*)

    Felicity, at present changing her Hammond Innes. We had
    a terrible experience coming down. We had to move our
    compartment three times to avoid a clergyman who was
    looking up her legs under cover of the *Daily Telegraph*.

MRS. WICKSTEED: And such a respectable newspaper.

LADY RUMPERS: I lie awake at night in a cold sweat wondering
    what would happen if Felicity's body fell into the wrong
    hands.

MRS. SWABB: But this is a doctor's. Doctors can touch anybody,
    because they don't have the feelings to go with it. That's
    what they go to medical school for.

LADY RUMPERS: Rubbish. Doctors are as bad as anyone else. I
    could tell you of a doctor who once touched me and I will
    never forget it.

MRS. SWABB: There's no need to tell me, I know.

MRS. WICKSTEED: You know? How do you know?

MRS. SWABB: Because I am Fate. I cut the string.

    I know all goings out and comings in.
    Naught escapes me in a month of Sundays:
    I know if they change their undies.
    Hoover, hoover, hoover.
    Hoover, hoover, hoover.

Now a scene setting scene to set the scene and see the set,
set the scene up and see the set up.

WICKSTEED: A thorough examination? Are you ill?

THROBBING: Never felt better. Your sister, Connie and I are
about to get married.

WICKSTEED: She hasn't told me.

THROBBING: Probably because I haven't told her. But this is her
last chance. Ten years of courtship is carrying celibacy to
extremes.

WICKSTEED: Poor girl.

THROBBING: And I thought before I embarked on the choppy
waters of the *vita coniugalis* I'd better have the vessel
overhauled. If I can stretch my metaphor.

WICKSTEED: Ah well, drop your trousers.

THROBBING: What for?

WICKSTEED: The longer I practise medicine the more convinced
I am there are only two types of cases: those that involve
taking the trousers off and those that don't. I'm waiting.

THROBBING: I'm a bit shy.

WICKSTEED: Why? No one will come in.
(MRS. SWABB *instantly does so, as the* CANON *drops his trousers.
And pulls them up again.*)

MRS. SWABB: Hoover, hoover, hoover.

WICKSTEED: Get out.

MRS. SWABB: Hoover, hoover, hoover.

THROBBING: Couldn't I go behind a screen?

WICKSTEED: In the course of thirty-odd years in pursuit of the
profession of medicine, Canon Throbbing, a profession to
which I unwittingly yoked myself in my callow youth,
people have been taking their trousers off in front of me at
the average rate of five times a day, five days a week,
fifty-two weeks in the year. This means that at a conservative
estimate and allowing for some duplication I have seen
twenty-five thousand sets of private parts. The most
conscientious whore could not have seen more. In the light
of such statistics you are displaying not so much modesty as
arrogance. TAKE THEM OFF.
(THROBBING *goes off.*)

15

WICKSTEED: We were taught many things at medical school, padre, but seeing through several thick layers of winceyette was not one of them.

Off?

Yes.

Turn round.

Bend over.

Get any feelings of nausea at all?

THROBBING: No.

WICKSTEED: Well God knows I do. It's all guesswork you know. I delve in their ears, I peer up their noses. I am glued to every orifice of the body like a parlour-maid at a keyhole.

THROBBING: May I get up now?

WICKSTEED: Shut up. And so it goes on. Day after day. Week after week. They troop in with their sore throats and their varicose veins. They parade before me bodies the colour of tripe and the texture of junket. Is this the image of God, this sagging parcel of vanilla blancmange hoisted day after day on to the consulting-room table? Is this the precious envelope of the soul? Is this. . . .

THROBBING: Is this on the National Health?

WICKSTEED: No. Why do you want to get married, anyway?

THROBBING: Because . . . because I look up girls' legs.

WICKSTEED: Marriage won't stop that.

THROBBING: Won't it?

WICKSTEED: I'm afraid not.

THROBBING: You mean, you still do?

WICKSTEED: Me? No. I'm a doctor.

THROBBING: Well, I do, and I'm a clergyman.

WICKSTEED: My poor sister. Because she's flat-chested he thinks she's religious.

(THROBBING *climbs on his bicycle and exits.*)

CONNIE: I don't love him.

MRS. WICKSTEED: Love? You look on the shelf and you'll find it cluttered with dozens of spinsters gathering dust and all of them labelled "I was waiting for love". I married Arthur for love and what did I get? The mucky end of the stick. I could kick myself.

WICKSTEED: Do you know who I could have married?

MRS. WICKSTEED: Do you know who I could have married?

WICKSTEED: Sir Percy Shorter.

MRS. WICKSTEED: Sir Percy Shorter.

WICKSTEED: Twice the man Arthur ever was.

MRS. WICKSTEED: Twice the man Arthur ever was.

WICKSTEED: Or will be.

MRS. WICKSTEED: Or will be. I get to look more and more like the Queen Mother every day.

DENNIS: Mother.

MRS. WICKSTEED: Yes?

DENNIS: I've got some bad news.

MRS. WICKSTEED: Yes?

DENNIS: I've only got three months to live.

MRS. WICKSTEED: Three months? Two months ago you only had ten days.

DENNIS: I made a mistake.

MRS. WICKSTEED: And what's happened to the galloping consumption you had last Thursday? Slowed down to a trot I suppose. What is it this time?

DENNIS: I've got a very rare disease.

MRS. WICKSTEED: You've got an extremely common disease. You've got a dose of the can't help its. You'd better ask your father.

DENNIS: He doesn't care.

WICKSTEED: That's true enough.

DENNIS: It's called Brett's Palsy.

(*He shows her a medical book.*)

MRS. WICKSTEED: Tiredness, irritability, spots, yes. And generally confined to the Caucasus. If this germ is confined to the Caucasus what's it doing in Hove?

WICKSTEED: Over here for the hols, I suppose.

MRS. WICKSTEED: Tragic. And he came through puberty with such flying colours.

CONNIE: Every day and in every way they're getting bigger and bigger and bigger.

DENNIS: I'm going to die, Connie.

CONNIE: Every day and in every way they're getting bigger and bigger and bigger.

DENNIS: I'm dying and no one will believe me.

MRS. SWABB: Listen to this. "Lucille is from Sydenham. Her hobbies are water-skiing and world peace."

DENNIS: That's my magazine.

MRS. SWABB: Someone hid it on top of the wardrobe.

CONNIE: If I had those I wouldn't need hobbies.

MRS. SWABB: No dear. Look. "Send off this postcard and a beautiful bust can be yours this summer for only £5."

DENNIS: Two fifty each.

CONNIE: False ones. Do you think so?

DENNIS: I would, Connie, if it were me.

MRS. WICKSTEED: Connie? Connie? Who's Connie? I've told you before, Dennis. Connie has a title. She's your Aunt Connie.

CONNIE: Aunt isn't a title.

MRS. WICKSTEED: It's the nearest you'll ever get to one. Calling your aunt by her Christian name. I knew a girl once who called her parents by their Christian names. She had a baby before she was seventeen. And what was the father called? She hadn't even bothered to ask. So much for names. (*Exits.*)

(MRS. SWABB *fills in the postcard.*)

CONNIE: It's no use. Look at my legs.

MRS. SWABB: Very nice legs, if you ask me. There are people running about with no legs at all, who'd be more than happy to have yours.

CONNIE: By rights with me it ought to be all lemon tea and neutered cats. But it isn't. I look like this on the outside but inside I feel like Jan Masefield.

MRS. SWABB: No, dear, Jayne Mansfield.

CONNIE: No. Jan Masefield. She was a girl in the front row at my school. Actually it was the second row but it looked like the front row.

MRS. SWABB: I'll post this postcard personally
    I'm sure it's for the best
    You wait she'll be a different girl
    With the Cairngorms on her chest.

DENNIS: Is that a lump there?

CONNIE: Yes.

DENNIS: Oh God.

CONNIE: Your fountain-pen. You want to say: look, this body doesn't really suit me. Could I move into something different? But you can't. The body's a tied cottage. At birth you're kitted out with mousey hair, bad legs, and no tits. . .

MRS. SWABB: That's right dear. You get it off your chest. Look out, it's the priest with five fingers.

THROBBING: Precious. Dr. Wicksteed's given me a clean bill of health. Isn't it wonderful?

DENNIS: I've got Brett's Palsy.

THROBBING: How interesting.

DENNIS: Three months to live.

THROBBING: As long as that? It's the green light, Connie.

DENNIS: She hasn't said yes yet.

THROBBING: With you sitting there she hasn't had much chance. Haven't you anything to do?

DENNIS: No.

THROBBING: If I had only three months to live I'd have a hundred and one things to do.

DENNIS: Like what?

THROBBING: Take my library books back, stop the papers, warn the milkman——

DENNIS: Death isn't like going away on holiday, you know.

THROBBING: Oh yes it is. It's going away for a long, long holiday to a place by all accounts every bit as nice as Matlock. For some of us anyway.

CONNIE: Dennis doesn't believe in heaven, do you Dennis?

DENNIS: No. I don't know what it means.

THROBBING: Nor did I till I met you, dearest. You'd better not sit near me. I've just been visiting the sick.

CONNIE: Dennis!

(*Exit* DENNIS *hurriedly.*)

THROBBING: Alone at last.

CONNIE: Yes.

THROBBING: Just you and me.

CONNIE: Yes.

THROBBING: The two of us.

CONNIE: Yes.

THROBBING: How old are you, Connie?

CONNIE: Thirty-three.

THROBBING: What a coincidence.

CONNIE: You're not thirty-three.

THROBBING: No, but my inside leg is. Oh, Connie.

CONNIE: Canon, please.

THROBBING: Forgive me: I was carried away. Connie. Will you marry me? Will you marry me?

MRS. SWABB: Right now it's make up your mind time for thirty-three-year-old "I keep myself to myself" Connie Wicksteed, a spinster from Brighton's Hove. Does she accept the hand of slim, balding "Just pop this in your offertory box" Canon Throbbing, no dish it's true, but with a brilliant future on both sides of the grave
or
does she give him the (*buzzer*) on the off-chance of something more fetching coming along once her appliance arrives?

CONNIE: Oh, Mr. Right, where are you? Just give me a few more days. Until Thursday.

THROBBING: Very well. After all, what is two more days in Purgatory if it's followed by a lifetime in Paradise?

WICKSTEED: You silly man. You silly woman. Handcuffing yourselves together. Don't do it. What for? I'd rather have a decent glass of sherry any day. Of course, I despise the body. Despise it. Stroking faces, holding hands, oh it all looks very nice on the surface, but look inside: the pipes are beginning to fur and the lungs to stiffen. We're all pigs, pigs; little trotters, little tails. Offal. Show me a human body and I will show you a cesspit.
(FELICITY *enters in a pool of rosy light and to shimmering music.*)
I eat every word.

FELICITY: I was passing the door and I came over rather faint.

WICKSTEED: I feel just the same. Is there anything I could offer you?

FELICITY: If I could just sit down.

WICKSTEED: Perhaps you would like some tea—or would you prefer me to clap my moist lips over yours and plunge my tongue again and again into your mouth sending you mad with desire—or would you prefer coffee?

FELICITY: Anything.

WICKSTEED: What is your name?

FELICITY: Felicity.

WICKSTEED: Felicity what?

FELICITY: The Hon. Felicity Rumpers.

WICKSTEED: Indeed? Connie, fetch in the delphiniums will you: I think we have a private patient.

FELICITY: I'm feeling much better now.

WICKSTEED: Are you?

FELICITY: I like it here.

WICKSTEED: Yes?

FELICITY: The atmosphere. The feel of the place.

WICKSTEED: I'm glad. It's . . . it's a bit untidy. It could do with smartening up a bit. Old, I suppose, without being old-fashioned. Carpets a bit thin. . . . Plumbing's a bit noisy sometimes too. Bit smelly, even. Tobacco. Drink. But I tell you: it's a good deal better than a lot of these cheap gimcrack things you could pick up these days, even if it is a bit run down.

FELICITY: Yes?

WICKSTEED: Yes.

(*The telephone rings.*)

Excuse me, Miss Rumpers, one moment. Hello. Dr. Wicksteed's surgery. Wicksteed speaking. Ah. Mr. Purdue. Yes. One moment. This is an interesting call Miss Rumpers, and one that illustrates how vital a part we doctors play in the community. I have always made a point of making myself available for anyone who cares to call, anyone in trouble, in despair, anyone in particular who is contemplating suicide.

FELICITY: Suicide!

WICKSTEED: This patient, Mr. Purdue, is on the brink of self-destruction. But before he actually attempts to take his own life, he calls me, his family doctor knowing I will be here.

FELICITY: The poor man.

WICKSTEED: A kind voice, a friendly word will often just tip that delicate balance between life and death, will turn back the patient from embarking on that journey to that far country from whose bourne, as Shakespeare so well put it, no traveller returns. So if you'll excuse me, I'll just have a word with him . . . strictly speaking of course I shouldn't, as you're a private patient and he isn't. . . .

FELICITY: No, no, not at all.

WICKSTEED: That's most magnanimous of you.

FELICITY: No. I'm quite happy.

WICKSTEED: Well I only wish Mr. Purdue was. Hello, Mr. Purdue. Mr. Purdue, hello . . . He seems to have . . . hung up. I am wondering whether I ought to give you a little examination.

MRS. WICKSTEED (*off*): Arthur!

WICKSTEED: Though now would not appear to be the best time. Excuse me one moment.

FELICITY: It used to be so flat. Can you tell?

> (*To the tune of "On the Isle of Capri".*)
> T'was on the A43 that I met him.
> We just had a day by the sea.
> Now he's gone, and he's left me expecting.
> Will somebody, please, marry me.

DENNIS: I didn't know anyone was here.

FELICITY: Hello.

DENNIS: I've got a disease called Brett's Palsy. I've only got three months to live.

FELICITY: Really?

DENNIS: Yes. At the outside.

FELICITY: But that's tragic.

DENNIS: I'm glad somebody thinks so.

FELICITY: You're so young.

DENNIS: Don't touch me. You're sure you haven't got any disease?

FELICITY: No, you have.

DENNIS: Yes, but I don't want any complications, do I?

FELICITY: You poor boy. Poor frightened boy.

DENNIS: Don't tell my father. He's a doctor.

FELICITY: Perhaps he could heal you.

DENNIS: Him? He couldn't heal a shoe.

FELICITY: This disease: you say there's no cure?

DENNIS: None.

FELICITY: And in three months you'll be dead?

DENNIS: I'm certain.

FELICITY: Look, I'd like to see you again. Can I?

DENNIS: Me? You must be peculiar.

FELICITY: I would, I would really.

DENNIS: When? I don't have much time.

FELICITY: Thursday 2.30. Where?

DENNIS: Here.

FELICITY: My name's Felicity. What's yours?

DENNIS: Dennis.

WICKSTEED: Trevor, what are you doing here. You've no business in the consulting room.

DENNIS: Good-bye, Penelope.

FELICITY: Felicity.

DENNIS: Yes.

WICKSTEED: My son, I'm afraid. Trevor.

FELICITY: He said his name was Dennis.

WICKSTEED: Did he? Then it probably is. Look, the doctor-patient relationship is such an important one, one of mutual trust and respect. And here are you such a young, shy innocent creature and I'm . . . somewhat older. It would be helpful, I think, it would help me, if we could break the ice a bit and maybe perhaps sometime go for a spin in the car sometime, anytime, say Thursday at 2.30?

FELICITY: My mother's very strict. I. . . .

WICKSTEED: Splendid, I'll meet you at the end of the West Pier.

MRS. WICKSTEED (off): Arthur!

WICKSTEED: You won't be late?

FELICITY: I'm never late.

WICKSTEED: Coming, my love.

> No. Not too old at fifty-three.
> A worn defeated fool like me.
> Still the tickling lust devours.

23

Long stretches of my waking hours.
Busty girls in flowered scanties
Hitching down St. Michael panties.
Easing off their wet-look boots,
To step into their birthday suits.
No! I am abusing my position
As their trusty old physician.
Virtue be mine, I will not do it
Just to pacify this lump of suet.

MRS. SWABB: I see it all. His ruse I rumble:
　　　　　That spotless girl he means to tumble.

MRS. WICKSTEED: Who was that?

WICKSTEED: Only a patient.

MRS. WICKSTEED: Man or woman.

WICKSTEED: They're all the same to me.

MRS. WICKSTEED: How old are we, Arthur?

WICKSTEED: You are fifty-one and I am. . . .

MRS. WICKSTEED: Fifty-three.

WICKSTEED: Fifty-three. And it doesn't seem five minutes since I
　　was sixteen.

MRS. WICKSTEED: When did the fire go out, Arthur?

WICKSTEED: What?

MRS. WICKSTEED: Nothing. It isn't as if he's attractive. I'm much
　　more attractive than he is. If he would only stretch out his
　　hand and say my name.

WICKSTEED: Muriel.

MRS. WICKSTEED: Yes.

WICKSTEED: It is your cake-decorating class on Thursday?

MRS. WICKSTEED: Yes. Why?

WICKSTEED: Then you won't be wanting the car.

MRS. WICKSTEED: No. Why?

WICKSTEED: I am going to the open session of the B.M.A.
　　Conference.

MRS. WICKSTEED: Indeed? The house will be empty.

WICKSTEED: I'll put an end to this duplicity . . .
　　　　　But not before I've had Felicity.
　　　　　Then take, oh take this itch away
　　　　　Lest my ruin end this play.

(*The telephone rings.*)

MRS. SWABB: Telephone. Telephone. Telephone.

MRS. WICKSTEED: Hello. Dr. Wicksteed's residence. Yes. Speaking. *Percy!*

MRS. SWABB: That will be Sir Percy Shorter to whom some reference has already been made.

MRS. WICKSTEED: After all these years! Longing to. Longing to. Well, why not here? Yes. Thursday afternoon. No. He's going out. Yes. How exciting. Yes. Mum's the word. Good-bye. Kiss, Kiss, Kiss.

MRS. SWABB: It is the afternoon of the Thursday in question, and, lunch, cooked by the fair hands of guess who is just over. I started them off with a little clear soup with scattered *croûtons*, followed by a fricassee of lamb with just a hint of rosemary. This I garnished with diced carrots and pommes duchesses. Then they had apple charlotte or the cheese board, followed by wafer thin mints and a choice of beverages. I think they enjoyed it.

WICKSTEED: It was disgusting.

(MRS. WICKSTEED *wears a dashing hat with perky feathers.*)

MRS. WICKSTEED: I think this hat suits me. Of course, it needs someone who can carry it off. You can't skulk about in a hat like this.

CONNIE (*in her cub mistress's uniform*): Has anyone seen my woggle?

MRS. SWABB: When did you have it last?

MRS. WICKSTEED: I should look in what is inappropriately in your case called your breast pocket.

MRS. SWABB: Here's another picture of Sir Percy addressing the conference.

WICKSTEED: He hasn't grown an inch in twenty years.

MRS. WICKSTEED: Size isn't everything.

(*The door bell rings.*)

DENNIS (*aside*): She's early!

MRS. WICKSTEED (*aside*): He's early!

DENNIS: ⎫
MRS. WICKSTEED: ⎬ I'll go.

MRS. SWABB: Stand back! I am the door. It's not a person. It's a parcel.

WICKSTEED: A parcel?

MRS. WICKSTEED: A parcel!

MRS. SWABB: A parcel! For Miss Wicksteed.

CONNIE: For me?

MRS. WICKSTEED: Yes.

CONNIE: I'm expecting it.

MRS. WICKSTEED: Who's it from?

CONNIE: I don't know.

MRS. WICKSTEED: You're expecting it and you don't know who it's from? I've never heard of that before.

WICKSTEED: I have. My surgery's full of girls expecting something and they don't know who it's from.

MRS. WICKSTEED: Most mysterious. Not that I'm in the least bit curious. (*Exits.*)

CONNIE: I think it's them.

MRS. SWABB: Open it.

CONNIE: I shan't dare wear them.

MRS. SWABB: Come on.

CONNIE: But it's time for cubs.

MRS. WICKSTEED: Mrs. Swabb, you may take the afternoon off.

MRS. SWABB: But I have an enormous backlog of dusting.

MRS. WICKSTEED: I insist . . . all work and no play makes Jack a dull boy. And talking of dull boys, what are your plans?

DENNIS: A long walk in the fresh air.

MRS. WICKSTEED: Splendid. And you?

CONNIE: Cubs. Why?

MRS. WICKSTEED: Just asking. I'm going to my cake-decorating class. I don't really want to, but we're electing a new secretary and it's like anything else: if the rank and file don't go the militants take over. (*Exits.*)
(*They open the parcel.*)

MRS. SWABB: "I was a spinster for fifteen years," writes Miss P.D. of Carshalton. Three years ago I invested in your appliance, and since then I have been engaged four times."

DENNIS: "The Rubens, in sensitized Fablon, as used on Apollo space missions." Try it on.

CONNIE: No. It's too late.

MRS. SWABB: It's never too late. Listen.

"In reply to yours. . . . Etc., etc. . . . They are easily
fitted without assistance but to forestall any difficulties our
fitter Mr. Shanks will call on Thursday May 29th."

DENNIS: That's today.

CONNIE: But he can't. I'm not here. I'm at cubs.

(MRS. WICKSTEED *claps hands offstage.*)

MRS. SWABB: Look out. Heads down.

CONNIE: What shall I do?

MRS. SWABB: Say you're ill.

MRS. WICKSTEED: Still hanging about? You should have been at
the toadstool half an hour ago! A scout is punctual at all
times. That was the rule when I was a scout.

DENNIS: She's ill.

MRS. WICKSTEED: She's late. Come along, clear the decks.
Off, off, off. Out, out, out.
Good-bye house, good-bye chairs . . . good-bye.

WICKSTEED: What's all the hurry? Anybody'd think you wanted
us out of the way.

MRS. WICKSTEED: Wanted you out of the way? What a ridiculous
idea! What an absurd idea! Why, the idea is absurd. It is
ridiculous. Relax. There's plenty of time. It's only 2.30.

WICKSTEED: 2.30. My God. 2.30. Plenty of time! Don't be
ridiculous. There's not a moment to lose.

(*He rushes out and they all follow.*)

MRS. SWABB: Quiet, isn't it? Gone quiet. It won't last. It will not
last. Give them five minutes and they'll be in and out of
here like dogs at a bazaar. Sniffety sniffety sniff. On the
fruitless quest of bodily pleasures. And it is all a waste of
time. After all as I tell my husband what is the body but
the purse of the soul? What is the flesh but the vest of the
spirit? Me, I don't bother with sex. I leave that to the
experts.

(DENNIS *and* FELICITY *come in.*)

DENNIS: Hello.

FELICITY: Hello, Dennis.

DENNIS: You remembered my name, Penelope.

FELICITY: Felicity.

DENNIS: I'm supposed to be out for a long walk in the fresh air.

FELICITY: I'm supposed to be meeting your father. What are you staring at?

DENNIS: Nothing. You.

FELICITY: Me? What for?

DENNIS: You're so nice looking, firm and full whereas. . . .

FELICITY: Your poor hands. All those long thin fingers.

DENNIS: See all the veins. Horrible.

FELICITY: I don't mind.

DENNIS: Don't you honestly?

FELICITY: Girls don't. They don't expect all that much. That's the first lesson you've got to learn. Most men don't bear close examination.

DENNIS: You seem to know a lot about it. I know nothing. I've got such a lot to learn.

FELICITY: And so little time to learn it.

DENNIS: And nobody to teach me. I was wondering . . .

FELICITY: Yes?

DENNIS: Could we go for a walk?

FELICITY: It's too hot for walking.

DENNIS: Yes. I suppose it is.

FELICITY: Of course, we could walk a little . . . then throw ourselves down in some lush warm summer-scented meadow.

DENNIS: I get hay fever.

FELICITY: Or pause by a sparkling stream and perch together on some cool moss-grown rock.

DENNIS: I get piles.

FELICITY: Nature is hard.

DENNIS: I could take my raincoat.

FELICITY: What a brilliant idea.

DENNIS: Felicity.

FELICITY: What?

DENNIS: I feel very peculiar. I think I may be catching something.

(*They take hands and go.*)

MRS. SWABB: Bless them! I think they've clicked. Scorpio and

Sagittarius. Lovely combo. Well, I think I'll just have a glance at the *Lancet*.

(*Enter* MRS. WICKSTEED.)

MRS. WICKSTEED: You!

MRS. SWABB: The mistress of the house! I wasn't expecting your return.

MRS. WICKSTEED: No, I have returned unexpectedly. An unforeseen hitch at my cake-decorating class! A shortage of hundreds and thousands put paid to the proceedings. Anyway, I thought I gave you the afternoon off.

MRS. SWABB: I am an indefatigable worker.

MRS. WICKSTEED: You are a Nosy Parker. If you're so anxious to be doing something, there's one or two groceries waiting to be picked up.

MRS. SWABB: Where?

MRS. WICKSTEED: Sainsbury's, where else? That takes care of her for the next two hours.

(*Exit* MRS. WICKSTEED *and* MRS. SWABB.)

(*Sea sounds.*)

WICKSTEED (*alone*): Break, break, break

> On thy cold grey stones, O Sea
> And would that my tongue could utter
> The thoughts that arise in me.

Would that it could, but you see Felicity I'm rather a shy person.

Are you Doctor?

Don't call me Doctor. Call me Arthur.

Are you Arthur?

Now you mention it, Felicity, I suppose I am. But you Felicity . . . you somehow restore my faith in human kind, remind me of what perfection the human body is capable. And spirit, oh yes, and spirit, Felicity. To think I was already qualified when you were born. I might have brought you into the world, felt the first flutter of your fragrant life. I could have cradled you in my arms, touched your little face. . . .

Arthur.

Yes, Felicity?

Arthur, you could still.
Could I? Oh, Felicity. (*Exits.*)
(*The door chimes go.*)
(*Enter* MR. SHANKS.)

MRS. WICKSTEED: Percy. . . . Oh, good afternoon.

SHANKS: I'm looking for someone by the name of Wicksteed.
W-I-C-K-S-T-E-E-D. Wicksteed. Yes.

MRS. WICKSTEED: Yes?

SHANKS: And I think I've found her. Mr. Shanks is the name.
Full marks. Ten out of ten. They are wonderful. *Wonderful.*

MRS. WICKSTEED: You think so?

SHANKS: They are outstanding. Out-standing.

MRS. WICKSTEED: Golly. Appreciation after all these years.

SHANKS: What a charming home, and my goodness, don't they
enhance it. The balance, dear lady, almost perfect. Almost,
but not quite. Still, that's what I'm here for. May I?

MRS. WICKSTEED: This is what they must mean by the
Permissive Society.

SHANKS: I believe this one is a fraction bigger than the other.

MRS. WICKSTEED: To hell with symmetry. How that touch revives
me.

SHANKS: It will not have escaped your notice that the customer,
Miss Wicksteed, is becoming a little excited.

MRS. WICKSTEED: At last! A tenant for my fallow loins.

SHANKS: However, rest assured. This excitement is not mutual.
I am an expert. A crash course at Leatherhead, the firm's
training centre, set in the heart of Surrey's famous rural
surroundings, lays down a standard procedure for every
eventuality. Mind you, these are exceptional. I've only seen
one pair to rival these, and she's now the manageress of the
only cinema in Fleetwood. Look, you're such an outstanding
example, we often compare notes, my colleagues and I . . .
and since I've got my little Polaroid handy. . . .

MRS. WICKSTEED: I was wondering when you were going to
mention that. Your Polaroid, your lovely little Polaroid. . . .

SHANKS: Some snaps . . . just for the record. . . .

MRS. WICKSTEED: Yes, yes, a record. Music!
(*The stage is flooded with sensual music.*)

Muriel Wicksteed, what are you doing? Can this be you? Yes. Yes, it is me. The real me. The me I've always been deep down. Suddenly the body reasserts itself, breaks through the dead crust of morality, and from the chrysalis convention bursts the butterfly, freedom.

(*The telephone rings.*)

I will see to that. Dr. Wicksteed's residence. Oh, it's you Mr. Purdue. No, you cannot speak to Dr. Wicksteed. This is his afternoon off. You're about to commit suicide? I see. If you must choose to commit suicide on doctor's afternoon off, that's your funeral. *Au revoir*. Or I suppose I should say good-bye. Now where was I . . . Oh yes.

(*She embraces* SHANKS.)

SHANKS: I repeat there is nothing to be ashamed of. This is all in a day's work to me.

MRS. WICKSTEED: I don't think he should throw his promiscuity in my face. One doesn't like to think one is simply a convenience.

SHANKS: A client not a convenience.

MRS. WICKSTEED: Client? I'm not going to have to pay you for this?

SHANKS: It's all included in the five pounds.

MRS. WICKSTEED: Five pounds! That's wicked.

SHANKS: There's nothing more I can do.

MRS. WICKSTEED: He comes in here goes for my bust like a bull at a gate and then says there's nothing more he can do. There is more. "The bust is but the first port of call on the long voyage of love."

SHANKS: I have other ladies to see.

MRS. WICKSTEED: Other ladies. The idea!

SHANKS: Stop. Take them off. They are a sacred trust. You are not fit to wear them.

(*He slaps her bust.*)

SHANKS: It's the . . . it's the real thing, isn't it? Flesh.

MRS. WICKSTEED: Of course it's flesh. What did you think it was —blancmange?

SHANKS: Is there anywhere I could wash my hands?

MRS. WICKSTEED: Time enough to wash your hands when we've

been to Paradise and back.

SHANKS: No!

MRS. WICKSTEED: No. That means yes. So much at least Freud
has taught us.

She drags SHANKS *off*.)

(*Sea sounds.*)

WICKSTEED: It shocks you, I'm afraid, me a respectable,
middle-aged doctor waiting like a fool on the end of
Brighton Pier. Ludicrous? But listen.

Say nobody saw and nobody heard
Say no one at all would breathe a word
Say nobody knew the you that was you
And your secret dreams could all come true.
Picture the scene, figurez-vous,
You could have whoever you wanted to:
Felicity Rumpers, Omar Sharif,
Julie Andrews, Mr. Heath.
Orgies of swapping, five in a bed.
You, me and Omar, Julie and Ted.
Don't tell me you wouldn't, given the choice
Old men with schoolgirls, ladies with boys
If she's what I fancy you really can't quarrel,
'Cos given the chance you'd be just as immoral.
Nobody's perfect: I'm fifty-three.
And the tide's going out, Arthur Wicksteed, M.D.
(*Exits.*)

(*Enter* SHANKS *pursued by* MRS. WICKSTEED.)

SHANKS: No, no, please, no.

MRS. WICKSTEED: I am Diana. You are my quarry. I am stalking
you with all the lithe grace of a panther.

SHANKS: Does anyone know the dialling code for Leatherhead?

MRS. WICKSTEED: I close in for the kill, my haunches taut, my
flanks rippling. . . .

SHANKS: No, no.

MRS. WICKSTEED: My head goes down and I pounce.

SHANKS: Yee-ow.

(SHANKS *makes a run for it, straight into the arms of* SIR

PERCY.)

SIR PERCY: I'm looking for Mrs. Wicksteed.

MRS. WICKSTEED: Percy! Don't you recognize me?

SIR PERCY: Muriel. You haven't changed. She's enormous.

MRS. WICKSTEED: Do you know each other?

SIR PERCY: No.

SHANKS: How do you do.

SIR PERCY: How do you do. I was wondering
    whether. . . .   } *together*

MRS. WICKSTEED: I suppose I ought to. . . .

SIR PERCY: Perhaps you would tell me. . . . } *together*

MRS. WICKSTEED: In case you're wondering. . . .

SHANKS: Er. . . .

SIR PERCY: Yes?

SHANKS: Nothing.

SIR PERCY: Muriel, this man isn't your husband?

MRS. WICKSTEED: Yes! No.

SIR PERCY: Ah. I saw no resemblance but twenty years is a long
    time.

MRS. WICKSTEED: It is, it is.

SIR PERCY: If he is not your husband, what is he doing in his
    shirt tails?

MRS. WICKSTEED: He's a patient.

SIR PERCY: A patient.

MRS. WICKSTEED: What did you think he was . . . my lover,
    ha ha ha.

SIR PERCY: Ha ha ha.

SHANKS: Ha ha ha.

SIR PERCY: What are you laughing at? You've got no trousers on.

SHANKS: I can explain that.

SIR PERCY: Did anyone ask you?

SHANKS: No.

SIR PERCY: Are you a private patient?

SHANKS: No.

SIR PERCY: Then shut up. Unbalanced?

MRS. WICKSTEED: Mad. He only called for his tranquillizers.

SIR PERCY: Don't worry. I have some with me.

SHANKS: You have to padlock your underpants when she's

around, I can tell you.

SIR PERCY: Really?

SHANKS: She's man mad.

MRS. WICKSTEED: Me. Ha. She laughed her scornful laugh.

SIR PERCY: Here, take these.

SHANKS: No.

SIR PERCY: I am President of the British Medical Association.
Take them.

SHANKS: No.

SIR PERCY: Very well Muriel, we must go intravenous.

(MRS. WICKSTEED *prepares a hypodermic.*)

SHANKS: She took my trousers off.

SIR PERCY: What for?

SHANKS: What for? What do people usually take other people's
trousers off for?

SIR PERCY: You tell me.

SHANKS: She wanted my body.

SIR PERCY: Your body. Your body? Thank you Muriel. In case
of doubt, just knock them out.

SHANKS: What?

SIR PERCY: When hackles rise, I tranquillize.

MRS. WICKSTEED: They do less harm if you keep them calm.

SIR PERCY: Hold him, Muriel.

SHANKS: No. No. All I want is to telephone Leatherhead.

(SIR PERCY *injects him.*)

SIR PERCY: This is the way we generally telephone Leatherhead.
That's it. Up you get.

SHANKS: Please. Does anyone know the dialling code for
Leatherhead?

(SHANKS *collapses.*)

SIR PERCY: Typical of your husband.

MRS. WICKSTEED: Arthur?

SIR PERCY: Leaving a patient running loose about the place.

MRS. WICKSTEED: It wasn't really his fault.

SIR PERCY: Slapdash. Inconsiderate. Don't suppose he's changed.

MRS. WICKSTEED: You haven't changed either. Have I?

SIR PERCY: I never liked him. He once said I was small. You
were a fool, Muriel.

34

MRS. WICKSTEED: What?

SIR PERCY: To throw yourself away on that little nobody. Still I suppose he makes you happy.

MRS. WICKSTEED: Arthur? He falls asleep as soon as his teeth hit the glass. Oh Percy.

SIR PERCY: Is he about, your husband? I'd quite like to see him. The years have doubtless taken their toll?

MRS. WICKSTEED: No. He's gone to the conference. The open session.

SIR PERCY: What open session? There is no open session today.

MRS. WICKSTEED: You're certain?

SIR PERCY: Of course. I am the President. How else could I be here.

(MRS. SWABB *enters with a wheeled basket of groceries.*)

MRS. WICKSTEED: You've been quick.

MRS. SWABB: I had a following wind.

MRS. WICKSTEED: Where is Dr. Wicksteed?

MRS. SWABB: Dr. Wicksteed? He's on the Pier. (*Exits.*)

MRS. WICKSTEED: I fear the worst.

SIR PERCY: Death?

MRS. WICKSTEED: Sex. And if I know him, he's with a patient.

SIR PERCY: A patient? Indeed! First item on the agenda—get your things on. Second, a visit to the Pier. Come on, buck up. And third, the ruin of a certain general practitioner.
(*He lifts the semi-conscious* SHANKS, *who hangs like a dummy in his arms.*)
Take careful note of all you see.

MRS. WICKSTEED: I will, I will, and who knows. . . .

SIR PERCY: Yes?

MRS. WICKSTEED: This may be a blessing in disguise.

SHANKS: Disguise.

MRS. WICKSTEED: I shall be free.

SHANKS: Free.

MRS. WICKSTEED: And together the future will be ours. (*Exits.*)

SHANKS: Ours.

SIR PERCY: No fear. But revenge, ha ha.

SHANKS: Ha ha.

SIR PERCY: After all these years.

SHANKS: All these years.

SIR PERCY: I think we need a booster.

SHANKS: Booster.

(SIR PERCY *exits carrying* SHANKS.)

(*Sea sounds.*)

WICKSTEED: As the sun went down on that long afternoon, a lean, distinguished figure might have been observed standing all of an hour at the end of the Pier. Several times he made as if to greet solitary ladies as they approached, but each time he fell back, disappointed and alone. (*Exits.*)

(*Enter* SIR PERCY.)

MRS. SWABB: Ah, I know who this is. I'll call her down, Mr. Shanks. She's upstairs. Miss Wicksteed, your visitor.

(CONNIE *enters, wearing her appliance.*)

CONNIE: Well? What do you think of them? Aren't they wonderful.

SIR PERCY: This must be what they mean by the Permissive Society.

CONNIE: They've been held up by the rail strike.

SIR PERCY: Is that what it is? You *are* Miss Wicksteed, aren't you?

CONNIE: Yes, why?

SIR PERCY: Her boldness rouses me strangely.

CONNIE: Touch them if you like, they're very firm. But I suppose you know that. (*As Sir Percy touches her, his trousers fall.*) I don't think you ought to get excited.

SIR PERCY: No?

CONNIE: Tell me, if someone were stroking them would they be able to tell the difference?

SIR PERCY: I don't follow.

CONNIE: Would they be satisfied?

SIR PERCY: In due course, I hope, yes. Suspenders, Miss Wicksteed, how nice to find someone keeping up with the old ways. Oh God, think of all the years I've wasted. This is the sort of woman I've been waiting for. Bold, provocative with an ardour equal to mine. Come, let me clasp your urgent young body. Kiss me. Again. You earth maiden, will you marry me?

CONNIE: And I've only had them on five minutes! This is what they must mean by the Permissive Society. Could I ask you something?

SIR PERCY: Yes.

CONNIE: Are you supposed to wash them?

SIR PERCY: You mean, you don't?

CONNIE: No. Not yet.

SIR PERCY: You mad Lawrentian Creature.

CONNIE: I'd thought of brushing them. I've got a wire brush that might do.

(SIR PERCY *follows her off*.)

THROBBING: Ah, a pair of trousers. Oxfam! Zambia will be so grateful.

(*Exit* CONNIE *and* SIR PERCY *tangoing across the stage*.)

THROBBING: But what is this? My bride to be in the arms of another man, and before we're even married.

(CONNIE *and* SIR PERCY *return, still tangoing,* CONNIE *leaves* SIR PERCY *and joins* THROBBING *at the end of the dance*.)

CONNIE: My fiancé.

SIR PERCY: She has fainted. Stand back. I am a doctor.

THROBBING: You don't look like a doctor to me. You haven't any trousers on. You look like a cad and a loose fish. Get away, bending over the prostrate body of my fiancée in your underclothes, that is my privilege.

SIR PERCY: Poor fool. She thought she could seduce me.

THROBBING: Seduce? Her? I have been engaged to Miss Wicksteed for ten years and she has never so much as laid a finger on me.

SIR PERCY: King Sex is a wayward monarch.

THROBBING: Come on, come on. Stand up and fight. Stand up.

SIR PERCY: I am standing up.

THROBBING: You'll probably want some handicap on account of your size.

SIR PERCY: What did you say?

THROBBING: I'm bigger than you are.

SIR PERCY: What gives you that idea?

THROBBING: One doesn't exactly have to be a quantity surveyor. Little squirt.

SIR PERCY (*he lands a blow*): LITTLE.

THROBBING: Ooh. Ahh. Look. Can't we just talk this over? I've known quite a lot of small people in my time.

SIR PERCY: Small. Small.

THROBBING: I don't hold anybody's size against them. We don't know how big Shakespeare was, do we? And look at Hitler. Mind you, he's a bad example. Connie, are you all right?

CONNIE: Yes.

THROBBING: Has this man been interfering with you?

CONNIE: Yes. Yes oh yes. I'm going to marry him.

THROBBING: *Him?*

SIR PERCY: Why not, sailor?

CONNIE: Yes, why not? He found in me something I never knew was there.

THROBBING: Connie. What are those?

CONNIE: They're a recent development.

THROBBING: What is his name?

CONNIE: I haven't asked.

THROBBING: You're going to marry him and you don't even know his name?

CONNIE: Yes, I do know his name. His name is curtains billowing wide on a summer night. His name is a special secret rose pressed in an old book. His name is the name of all lovers down the ages who have cried their challenge to the wild night and dared to cast themselves away on the frail bark of love. What is your name, by the way?

SIR PERCY: Sir Percy Shorter.

(CONNIE *screams and exits.*)

It's not my fault if I send women mad.

THROBBING: Mad? You? You Mickey Mouse. Why don't you marry someone your own size? Goodness! It's time for Evensong.

SIR PERCY: That settles it. You're a clergyman. Start saying your prayers!

(DENNIS *and* FELICITY *come in with* MRS. SWABB.)

MRS. SWABB: Canon Throbbing, I don't think you know Miss Rumpers, newly returned from Addis Ababa.

THROBBING: Welcome to our shores.

(SIR PERCY *primes his hypodermic.*)

FELICITY: What are you doing?

SIR PERCY: The balance of his mind is disturbed. I am about to redress it.

(*Exit* THROBBING *pursued by* SIR PERCY.)

FELICITY: How do you think it will happen, then?

DENNIS: I imagine you just sort of fade away really. Don't lets talk about it.

FELICITY: How tragic. A widow at twenty-two.

DENNIS: I don't want to think about it any more.

FELICITY: No. I too will be brave. I will be more than brave. I will be plucky. "Felicity, his plucky young wife survives him."

DENNIS: All the germs will flee before the greatest medicine of them all.

FELICITY: Love?

DENNIS: Sex.

(*To the tune of* "*Shuffle off to Buffalo*".)

DENNIS: We'll be going rather steady
     So it's time to go to beddy
     Turn the lights down low.

FELICITY: Oh, oh, oh.

DENNIS: You know which way we're heading
     We're heading for a wedding.

MRS. SWABB: Oh no, no, no, no NO?

DENNIS: ⎱ "Some day the stork will pay a visit
MRS. SWABB: ⎰ and leave a little souvenir.

DENNIS: Just a little cute what is it.

FELICITY: We'll discuss that later, dear."

DENNIS: You go home and get your knickers
     And I'll race you to the vicar's
     And it's ends away.

FELICITY: ⎱
DENNIS: ⎰ Mm, mm, mm.

MRS. SWABB: Don't anticipate it
     Wait to consummate it
     Not every day's a wedding day.

(DENNIS *kisses her passionately.*)

DENNIS: You put your tongue in my mouth. Are you supposed

39

to do that?

FELICITY: It's optional.

DENNIS: This is what they must mean by the Permissive Society. Penelope.

FELICITY: Felicity.

WICKSTEED: Ah! Is this your long walk in the fresh air?

DENNIS: It's all right.

WICKSTEED: All right? you lay your acned face in Miss Rumpers' lap (Good afternoon, Miss Rumpers) and you say it's all right.

DENNIS: She doesn't mind. It's mutual.

WICKSTEED: Mutual! HA! It is never mutual. Get off. Get off. Be careful, I implore you, Miss Rumpers. That head is riddled with dandruff. Get out, you lounge lizard. You're not fit to hold a candle to Miss Rumpers, let alone anything else. My dear young lady, how can you forgive me? In my own house. . . .

FELICITY: Dennis and I. . . .

WICKSTEED: Stop! Stop! Do not couple your name with his. That he should even contemplate touching your fresh, clean, innocent, young body fills me with such shame, such loathing. Filth, filth. Forgive me.

FELICITY: No. Do not touch me.

WICKSTEED: No. How can I approach you? How can I even speak to you? The least thing about you, the spent cartridge of your lipstick, the dry bed of your compact, the fluff in your handbag's bottom, all the fragrant clutter of your loveliness, I am as dirt and vileness beside it. *But.* . . .

FELICITY: But?

WICKSTEED: But speaking thus I speak as a man. And as a man I cannot touch you, but as a doctor . . .

FELICITY: Does that make a difference?

WICKSTEED: Oh yes. As a man I see you as a fresh, lovely, passionate creature. As a doctor, you are to me a machine, an organism, a mere carcass. Feeling does not enter into it. As a doctor I am a eunuch: I touch you . . . without passion, and without desire.

FELICITY: Yes.

40

WICKSTEED: Now I touch you as a man.

FELICITY: Yes.

WICKSTEED: Now I touch you as a doctor.

FELICITY: Yes.

WICKSTEED: You see the difference? So have no fears, my dear
young lady when in a few moments I shall ask you to
remove your clothes in their entirety. Because I shall be as
far from desire as is a plumber uncovering a manhole. Off.
Off.

(FELICITY *goes off*.)

How well I understand your fears. Life is such a dirty
business these days. Everyone trying to grab what he can.
What is the poem. . . .

FELICITY: I don't know.

WICKSTEED: A young Diana golden haired,
      Stands dreaming on the verge of strife,
      Magnificently unprepared.
      For the long littleness of life.
      Are you prepared for that, Felicity?
      The long littleness . . . sometimes longer,
      sometimes littler
      It comes as quite a shock to some girls . . .
      others just take it in their stride.

(FELICITY *enters in her slip*.)

Hello.

(*He kisses her*.)

      Hello ears.
      Hello eyes.
      Hello nose.
      Hello mouth.
      Hello fingers.
      Hello knees.
      Hello Percy.

(SIR PERCY *has come in and is watching aghast*.)

SIR PERCY: So.

WICKSTEED: I was just giving this young lady an aspirin.

SIR PERCY: In her underclothes?

FELICITY: It's very hot in here.

41

WICKSTEED: Don't worry. I have a diploma in tropical medicine. Felicity, Miss Rumpers I don't think you know Sir Percy Shorter.

WICKSTEED:
SIR PERCY: } President of the British Medical Association.

SIR PERCY: Is this young lady a patient of yours?

WICKSTEED: The idea that a doctor of my reputation would meddle with a patient is repugnant to me. Leave my ears alone will you dear. And if not a patient, what?

SIR PERCY: You tell me.

WICKSTEED: A friend. Of the family. The whole family. Like you. Strange, because she's not a bit like you. Come out of there, Miss Rumpers. Nothing in my trousers pocket of any interest to you. Humbugs, you know. She knows I keep them there.

SIR PERCY: You're old enough to be her father.

WICKSTEED: So are you.

SIR PERCY: She wasn't tickling my ears.

WICKSTEED: That's true, Miss Rumpers, why don't you tickle Percy's ears. I don't think she wants to. I'm not surprised.

SIR PERCY: Enough of this. Shall I tell you what I think?

WICKSTEED: No.

FELICITY: Yes.

SIR PERCY: I think this young woman is a patient. That you were abusing your position to interfere with her. That it is a scandal. That you are a blackguard. That is is my duty to bring your little games to the notice of the Medical Disciplinary Committee. That I will do all in my power to have you struck off.

WICKSTEED: No.

SIR PERCY: What have you to say to that?

WICKSTEED: You little pratt.

SIR PERCY: WHO ARE YOU CALLING LITTLE?

(MRS. WICKSTEED *enters*.)

MRS. WICKSTEED: Arthur!

WICKSTEED: Muriel!

SIR PERCY: I have just discovered your husband with his tongue

42

down this young lady's throat.

MRS. WICKSTEED: Kissing. Kissing. You slut!

SIR PERCY: I fear kissing was just the tip of the iceberg.

MRS. WICKSTEED: Of course I've known for years our marriage has been a mockery. My body lying there night after night in the wasted moonlight. I know now how the Taj Mahal must feel.

WICKSTEED: Listen. I can explain everything.

MRS. WICKSTEED: No. Save it for the decree nisi.

WICKSTEED: Divorce? We can't get divorced. Think of our son, Trevor.

MRS. WICKSTEED: DENNIS.

WICKSTEED: He will be the child of a broken home. He will probably turn to juvenile delinquency.

MRS. WICKSTEED: He is too old for juvenile delinquency.

WICKSTEED: Thank God for that.

MRS. WICKSTEED: Mention of divorce and avenues open up all round. Think of it, Percy: a hostess, perhaps at one of our leading London hotels, catering for an international clientele, where my knowledge of languages can be put to good use.

WICKSTEED: You have no knowledge of languages.

MRS. WICKSTEED: A smile knows no frontiers. Thank goodness I'm not alone.

WICKSTEED: And now, suddenly, at this moment of rejection, she goes knock, knock, knock at the door of my heart, and through a gap in the chintz I see the ghost of an old passion.

SIR PERCY: Come, Muriel, lean on me.

(*Enter* PURDUE *with a ready noosed rope.*)

PURDUE: Excuse me, Doctor. . . .

WICKSTEED: I'm sorry, Mr. Purdue. It's my afternoon off. I have lost my career. I have lost my wife. You are all I've got left.

FELICITY: Me?

WICKSTEED: Yes. But we can be happy together, you and I. Together we can defy the world. Snap our fingers at public opinion. What do you say, Felicity?

(PURDUE *is meanwhile preparing to hang himself.*)

DENNIS: Can I help, Mr. Purdue?

PURDUE: Nobody can help me.

43

DENNIS: Oh, don't say that.

SIR PERCY: I won't mention my engagement for the moment. She'll understand, of course. Sensible girl. Never been the clinging type.

PURDUE: I'm going to do it.

MRS. WICKSTEED: Come, Percy. Come into the house of my body. Shelter from the storms of life under the eaves of my breasts.

PURDUE: I am going to do it.

WICKSTEED: What do you say?

FELICITY: Actually, I'm already spoken for.

WICKSTEED: Spoken for? By whom?

FELICITY: Dennis.

WICKSTEED: Dennis? Who's Dennis?

FELICITY: Your son, Dennis.

WICKSTEED: Leonard! O my God!

PURDUE: I'm going to do it. I am really.

MRS. WICKSTEED: What are you doing standing on my best chair?

PURDUE: Oh, sorry.

(MRS. WICKSTEED *removes the chair, leaving* PURDUE *hanging.*

DENNIS *and* FELICITY *are clasped in each other's arms as. . . .*)

MRS. SWABB (*announces*): Delia, Lady Rumpers.

LADY RUMPERS: Felicity!

CURTAIN

ACT TWO

MRS. WICKSTEED: We were just going to have a glass of sherry.

LADY RUMPERS: So I see.

WICKSTEED: You are Felicity's mother?

LADY RUMPERS: I am.

(LADY RUMPERS *looks fixedly at* PURDUE *who is still swinging*.)

WICKSTEED: Take no notice. Some people will do anything for effect.

(*He swings* PURDUE *on to a chair where he stands with his head still in the noose*.)

PURDUE: I don't really want to commit suicide. It's just a call for help.

LADY RUMPERS: So. I see I got here in the nick of time. Felicity, put that young man's hand back where it belongs and get some clothes on.

FELICITY: Yes, Mother.

LADY RUMPERS: Who is that depressing youth?

WICKSTEED: My son. He depresses me too.

LADY RUMPERS: Not too depressed to take my daughter's clothes off.

WICKSTEED: No, you worm.

MRS. WICKSTEED: He didn't.

WICKSTEED: Take no notice of my wife. She is his mother.

LADY RUMPERS: And you are his father.

WICKSTEED: Don't remind me.

SIR PERCY: Wicksteed did it. He is the culprit.

WICKSTEED: Yes. Yes. I did it. I am his father. I turned him into this, this snivelling loathsome, little lecher. Where did I go wrong, where do we go wrong, we parents, generation after generation?

45

SIR PERCY: It's all lies. I can tell you what happened. I don't believe we've had the pleasure.

MRS. SWABB: Allow me. This is Delia, Lady Rumpers.

SIR PERCY: Another titled person. What a breath of fresh air. Lady Rumpers, I am a doctor.

LADY RUMPERS: Another doctor. Then I don't want to hear another word. I've had a bellyful of doctors.

PURDUE: I want a doctor: I'm depressed.

MRS. WICKSTEED: So would I be if I had my head in a noose.

PURDUE: I only want to put *one* foot in the grave.

LADY RUMPERS: Oh, this is intolerable. Felicity. It shouldn't take all day for you to get your skirt on.

WICKSTEED: Can I help?

LADY RUMPERS: Don't touch her.

WICKSTEED (*to* DENNIS): No, get back. You've done enough damage.

DENNIS: Me?

WICKSTEED: Control yourself.

LADY RUMPERS: Daring so much as even to look at a girl like Felicity.

WICKSTEED: Yes.

MRS. WICKSTEED: No.

LADY RUMPERS: You are dirt.

WICKSTEED: Dirt.

LADY RUMPERS: Filth.

WICKSTEED: Filth.

FELICITY: Mother. He's sick.

WICKSTEED: Yes, sick; sick, sick. You toad.

SIR PERCY: If you'd allow me. . . .

WICKSTEED: Shut your face.

DENNIS: Dad. Dad.

WICKSTEED: Don't "Dad, Dad" me.

LADY RUMPERS: To think we've only been in this country three weeks. Everywhere it's the same. Sex, sex, sex. Well I'm not having any.

MRS. SWABB: I'm not surprised.

LADY RUMPERS: When I get you back to our suite at the Claremont, you're going straight into a hot bath and I shall

46

personally scrub you all over with carbolic.

WICKSTEED: Ah, the privileges of motherhood.

LADY RUMPERS: Perhaps you will believe me now, Felicity. Men will touch you, rob you, rifle you of all you possess.

SIR PERCY: Flesh isn't property, you know.

LADY RUMPERS: Yes it is. What is one's body but property? What is one's own flesh and figure but the most precious inheritance? When that is spent one is indeed bankrupt of everything. From this moment on I shall not let her out of my sight. Haile Selassie was right. We should never have left Addis Ababa.

(*Exit* LADY RUMPERS *and* FELICITY.)

MRS. WICKSTEED: You slid out of that very well.

WICKSTEED: I did rather.

MRS. WICKSTEED: I want you out of this house in half an hour.

WICKSTEED: Yes. I must collect my thoughts and pack.

MRS. WICKSTEED: And we must have a little talk, Percy. About the future.

SIR PERCY: Yes.

MRS. WICKSTEED: Our future.

(*Exit* SIR PERCY *and* MRS. WICKSTEED.)

PURDUE: Has everybody gone?

MRS. SWABB: Everybody of any consequence.

PURDUE: Marvellous!

MRS. SWABB: It's all self, self, self in this house. Locked in our tiny domestic tragedies only I, Amelia Swabb, can take the wider view. What seems to be the trouble?

PURDUE: I'm depressed.

MRS. SWABB: Pisces is in the second quarter of Saturn: naturally you're depressed.

PURDUE (*getting down*): I am Pisces.

MRS. SWABB: Why don't you look on the bright side? Next week the sun'll be in Saturn and Pisceans will be laughing.

(*Exit* MRS. SWABB *and* PURDUE.)

SIR PERCY: I have no sympathy with him at all. None.

MRS. WICKSTEED: He *is* my husband.

SIR PERCY: I do not understand how he could betray such a fine body. . . .

47

MRS. WICKSTEED: Nor do I.

SIR PERCY: As the British Medical Association.

MRS. WICKSTEED: What more does he want.

(*Enter* WICKSTEED.)

WICKSTEED: Not more. Different. (*Exits*.)

SIR PERCY: And a doctor. Entrusted with the bodies of his patients. Caught red-handed.

MRS. WICKSTEED: Red-handed, yours so plump and white.

SIR PERCY: Please, Muriel. Of course we have all been tempted. Every doctor has. The lowliest locum in the back streets of Liverpool can take advantage of a patient, if he allows himself. Because the doctor-patient relationship is itself a kind of seduction. But one says, "No. No, body, I will not do this. No, hands, keep to your appointed task. No, eyes, stick to the affected part." That is what Professionalism means. Yes?

MRS. WICKSTEED: Have you. . . .

SIR PERCY: Never, NEVER. Though I've had my chances. Discerning women seem to find me attractive, God knows why. . . .

MRS. WICKSTEED: Yes.

SIR PERCY: Look, Muriel, there's something I have to tell you. Walk tall, Percy.

MRS. WICKSTEED: Yes?

SIR PERCY: This afternoon . . . I met the woman of my dreams.

MRS. WICKSTEED: Oh Percy. (*Kisses him*.)

THROBBING: Good evening.

MRS. WICKSTEED: Canon Throbbing! I want you to be the first to know, Arthur apart. And it will be Arthur apart. Separation City, I'm afraid. You must congratulate us.

THROBBING: You and him? I think you must be mistaken. This man is engaged to my fiancée, Miss Wicksteed.

MRS. WICKSTEED: No, you are mistaken. You are engaged to your fiancée Miss Wicksteed.

THROBBING: That's what I thought until this afternoon.

MRS. WICKSTEED: This afternoon. What happened this afternoon?

THROBBING: I was present when he proposed.

MRS. WICKSTEED: Percy and Connie?

THROBBING: *He* proposed. She accepted. I protested. Then I had to get my skates on for Evensong.
(*Enter* WICKSTEED.)

WICKSTEED: Evensong on ice? The Church must be desperate. (*Exits.*)

MRS. WICKSTEED: Percy. Are you or are you not engaged to my sister-in-law?

SIR PERCY: Is your sister-in-law a woman with a nondescript face, but an outstanding figure?

MRS. WICKSTEED: Certainly not. She has a bust like a billiard table

THROBBING: She is as slim and graceful as a boy. Perhaps that is what attracted me to her in the first place.
(*Enter* WICKSTEED.)

WICKSTEED: Sometimes I think Freud died in vain. (*Exits.*)

SIR PERCY: Certainly a person purporting to be Miss Wicksteed thrust herself on me this afternoon. I can still feel her urgent young body rippling beneath my fingers.

MRS. WICKSTEED: It's unlike Connie to thrust herself, even slightly.

THROBBING: He must have led her on.

SIR PERCY: It's animal magic.

THROBBING: It's being little. They have to assert themselves.

SIR PERCY: Watch it, Vicar. I gave your sister-in-law no encouragement at all.

THROBBING: Then kindly explain, Lofty, how you came to be without your trousers.

MRS. WICKSTEED: Percy. Is this true?

SIR PERCY: No. Yes. President of the BMA, physician to the Queen: I can have any girl I want.

MRS. WICKSTEED: Connie. Come here this minute.
(CONNIE *enters, but without her appliance*).

CONNIE: Yes, Muriel.

MRS. WICKSTEED: Don't Muriel me, you minx. You seem to have been busy this afternoon. Now Percy. Is this the lady?

SIR PERCY: In some respects, yes. But what has happened to her urgent young body? I have been deceived. Terribly deceived. I don't want her either.

MRS. WICKSTEED: Now Connie. Perhaps you can throw some light on the proceedings. Canon Thing here has got it into his head that you are all washed up. Is this true?

CONNIE: Yes.

THROBBING: No. Oh Mowgli, my wild jungle child, say it's not true.

CONNIE: It is true.

MRS. WICKSTEED: Then who are you engaged to?

CONNIE: To this gentleman here. He proposed to me.

SIR PERCY: Lies. LIES, LIES, ALL LIES.

MRS. WICKSTEED: Are you sure he proposed?

CONNIE: Quite sure: he took his trousers off.

SIR PERCY: May I speak. MAY I SPEAK.

MRS. WICKSTEED: Percy.

SIR PERCY: MAY I?

THROBBING: No.

SIR PERCY: Look here. I am Sir Percy Shorter, FRCS, FRCP.

CONNIE: How do you do. I'm sure we're going to be very happy.

SIR PERCY: We are not. WE ARE NOT. WE ARE NOT GOING TO BE HAPPY AT ALL. I deny it. I deny everything. And I will go on denying everything. You believe her? Her unsupported . . . and I mean unsupported word against mine. And you Muriel. Think of the times we've had together. Do they mean nothing to you? NOTHING? This cringing, flat-chested, dowdy little spinster. I am not going to throw myself away on that. It's all fantasy. A fantasy of frustration and loneliness and sadness and despair. And as such entirely DESPICABLE. I think you owe me an apology.

MRS. WICKSTEED: Percy. How could I have ever doubted your word.

SIR PERCY: And do you agree her talk was fantasy?

MRS. WICKSTEED: A tissue of lies.

SIR PERCY: Very well. I am big enough to overlook it.

THROBBING: Just one moment. Am I right in thinking you deny anything untoward occurred this afternoon?

SIR PERCY: Absolutely. Absolutely.

THROBBING: What time did you come here this afternoon?

(*The next sequence must be like a cross examination, very gentle and slow, then gradually increasing in speed leading to the fatal slip of the tongue.*)

SIR PERCY: About three.

THROBBING: About three?

SIR PERCY: About three.

THROBBING: About three. You came into this room?

SIR PERCY: I came into this room.

THROBBING: You're sure of that?

SIR PERCY: Of course I'm sure. Look here. . . .

THROBBING: Miss Wicksteed came in?

SIR PERCY: That is correct.

THROBBING: And you say you arrived about three?

SIR PERCY: That is correct.

THROBBING: And then you . . . what . . . talked?

SIR PERCY: Talked, chatted, made conversation.

THROBBING: She was wearing a blue dress, is that right?

SIR PERCY: That is correct.

THROBBING: So you arrived about three, came into this room, talked, chatted, made conversation. . . .

SIR PERCY: Talked, chatted, made conversation. . . .

THROBBING: And she was wearing a blue dress?

SIR PERCY: A blue dress.

THROBBING: She sat on the sofa?

SIR PERCY: She sat on the sofa.

THROBBING: You stood?

SIR PERCY: That is correct.

THROBBING: And you say you arrived about three? And came into this room?

SIR PERCY: Arrived about three, came into this room.

THROBBING: Talked, chatted, made conversation?

SIR PERCY: Talked, chatted, made conversation.

THROBBING: And she was in her blue dress?

SIR PERCY: And she was in her blue dress.

THROBBING: And what colour were her knickers?

SIR PERCY: Blue . . . no pink. Argh!

THROBBING: Thank you Sir Percy. That's all I wanted to know. I'm sorry Miss Wicksteed. Your witness.

MRS. WICKSTEED: So. You big story.

SIR PERCY: Muriel.

MRS. WICKSTEED: Don't Muriel me, you four foot Casanova.

SIR PERCY: You see, you see. It always has to come back to that.

MRS. WICKSTEED: All those years I've dreamed of you, the man I might have married.

SIR PERCY: All right, I wanted you once, but you spurned me and why? Because I was small. And your husband laughed. Well when I've finished with you you'll both be laughing on the other side of your faces. Little, small. So I'm small am I? Well I'll tell you something Muriel. You are not small. Not small at all. You are HUGE. ENORMOUS.

MRS. WICKSTEED: Stop it.

SIR PERCY: You think I fancied you? You!

MRS. WICKSTEED: You did, you did.

SIR PERCY: You great wardrobe. That model went out years ago.

MRS. WICKSTEED: Stop it. I'm ageless, do you hear, ageless.

SIR PERCY: And don't think you're going to trundle back to your snivelling little husband, and live happily ever after in your nice little provincial backwater. Because I am going to break him. BREAK HIM, do you hear? I've broken bigger men than that. And I'll do it again. Professional misconduct. Professional incompetence, interfering with patients . . . a list of charges as long as my arm.

THROBBING: Well that's not very long.

SIR PERCY: Watch it, Vicar.

CONNIE: Please don't do it. For my sake.

SIR PERCY: For your sake? What did you ever do for me, except pull the wool over my eyes?

CONNIE: It was nice while it lasted.

SIR PERCY: It was an illusion.

CONNIE: It always is.

SIR PERCY: No. I shall break him. He's had his chips.

MRS. WICKSTEED: No. No.

SIR PERCY: The party's over, Doctor. Curtains. This is the end of the line for you, Arthur Wicksteed, a general practitioner from Brighton's Hove.

MRS. WICKSTEED: The shame! The disgrace! The POVERTY!

SIR PERCY: Finita La Commedia, Arturo.

(*Exit* SIR PERCY, *followed by* MRS. WICKSTEED.)

CONNIE: So you see now, marriage is out of the question.

THROBBING: Is it?

CONNIE: Oh yes. What I have done, you can't forgive. This foul, foul thing.

THROBBING: It was only kissing.

CONNIE: No. One kiss and he could have had anything. It would always lie between us. No I am Damaged Goods.

THROBBING: I forgive you.

CONNIE: You mustn't. He mustn't.

THROBBING: I must. It is my principles.

CONNIE: I am a harlot. A Jezebel.

THROBBING: I know, I know.

CONNIE: A whore.

THROBBING: Oh Connie, how infinitely more desirable you are now. Can't you see, Connie, what vistas are opening up?

CONNIE: I think I can. Oh God.

THROBBING: Sin with him you can sin with me. I wanted you before. I want you twice as much now.

CONNIE: No, please, Harold, no.

THROBBING: Gently we can lead each other on as together we explore all the alleys and pathways of the body. Just think of it.

CONNIE: I'm trying not to.

THROBBING: Together we shall be in the forefront of Anglican sexuality. Perhaps I might even write a frank and fearless account of our activities for the *Church Times*. Oh such sin. Only it won't be sin because we shall be married, married and allowed to do what we want. Married and FREE.

CONNIE: Free?

THROBBING (*to the tune of* "*Shuffle off to Buffalo*"):

> I must go and tell the verger
> That there'll shortly be a merger
> And it's some day soon.

CONNIE: No, no, no.

THROBBING: Can't believe my luck

> Because I'm going to break my duck
> Upon a honey, honey, honeymoon.

(*They exit as* MRS. WICKSTEED *and* MRS. SWABB *enter*.)

MRS. SWABB: It's kiss 'n' make up time. I'm glad to see somebody's doing the sensible thing. (*Exits*.)

MRS. WICKSTEED: Now, Muriel old girl. You're going to have to play your cards pretty carefully, or you will end up on the discard pile. I don't know. And me with the menopause just shoving its nose above the horizon. As if I didn't have enough on my plate.

(*Enter* WICKSTEED, *bags packed*.)

WICKSTEED: I fold up my twenty-five years in the medical profession. I put in twenty-odd years of marriage, plus a slightly threadbare respectability. And that's it. All in ten minutes. Ten minutes and the world turns. Our world. In Memphis, Tennessee, fourteen babies have been born since this play began. In Hobart, Tasmania, a flower turns to the sun. In Lima, Peru, an old man is dying, and in Birmingham, England, two lovers turn to each other in the silence of the night . . . and somewhere out there in the singing silence of space, a tin flag flutters. Our world. Somewhere between the loving and the lying and the kissing and the crying and the living and the dying and the fishing and the frying is that something we call life. Our world.

MRS. WICKSTEED: All packed, I see.

WICKSTEED: A few things I've thrown together.

MRS. WICKSTEED: Where are you going?

WICKSTEED: Relatives.

MRS. WICKSTEED: Close relatives?

WICKSTEED: Stevenage. I thing I have an aunt there.

MRS. WICKSTEED: You're a stinker, Arthur Wicksteed. Do you know that?

WICKSTEED: Oh yes.

MRS. WICKSTEED: A rotter.

WICKSTEED: It's funny. . . . Having you I didn't want you. Losing you, I want you again.

MRS. WICKSTEED: Hard cheese.

WICKSTEED: "His wife has promised to stand by him."

MRS. WICKSTEED: What?

WICKSTEED: I was just thinking, it would look better if you stood by me. Maybe I wouldn't be struck off.

MRS. WICKSTEED: It would *look* better. Of course I should have to dress the part: one thing I've learned in life is that few right thinking people can withstand a really good twin-set and pearls. But what about my feelings?

WICKSTEED: I was forgetting those.

MRS. WICKSTEED: As usual. After all she wasn't just something on the side, was she? There've been others.

WICKSTEED: A few.

MRS. WICKSTEED: A few?

WICKSTEED: Quite a few.

MRS. WICKSTEED: I am fed up.

WICKSTEED: I think I am too. Muriel. I suppose it's too late to start again.

MRS. WICKSTEED: Much too late. All those women lie between us.

WICKSTEED: And in your life, no one?

MRS. WICKSTEED: No one. Nothing. Never.

WICKSTEED: Percy?

MRS. WICKSTEED: A dream. A fantasy. No one has ever laid a finger on me except you. And you it's so long. I've almost forgotten. Suppose I were to overlook your disgraceful conduct.

WICKSTEED: My shameful, shameful conduct. Filthy conduct.

MRS. WICKSTEED: Yes.

WICKSTEED: If only you could be big enough.

MRS. WICKSTEED: Then there'd have to be a different going on.

WICKSTEED: How different?

MRS. WICKSTEED: No more twin beds.

WICKSTEED: I sleep so badly.

MRS. WICKSTEED: Then we shall sleep badly together.

WICKSTEED: Yes, Muriel.

MRS. WICKSTEED: Perhaps in the long watches of the night I shall bring you comfort.

WICKSTEED: Perhaps you will.

MRS. WICKSTEED: I will. There is no perhaps about it. You see, you have no rights, Arthur. They have been forfeited over the years. Whereas innocence has kept mine intact. Kiss me.

WICKSTEED: Here?

MRS. WICKSTEED: Yes. No. Hard.

WICKSTEED: If you insist.

(WICKSTEED *puts his arms round her and kisses her*.)

MRS. WICKSTEED: And that's how it's going to be. But I am not forcing you. You may take it or leave it.

WICKSTEED: This or my aunt in Stevenage. I suppose I'd better take it.

MRS. WICKSTEED: A wise decision. Now I think we might retire for a little nap.

WICKSTEED: But I'm not tired.

MRS. WICKSTEED: Excellent. Neither am I.

WICKSTEED: Muriel. I . . .

MRS. WICKSTEED: What?

WICKSTEED: Nothing.

MRS. WICKSTEED: You see, innocence will always triumph in the end.

WICKSTEED: Though if there was anybody I'd forgive you. I know.

MRS. WICKSTEED: No need. There was nobody. Nobody at all. Now, what were we talking about? The future.

WICKSTEED: No. The past.

MRS. WICKSTEED: Then we must listen to the voice of the future. (*Enter* SHANKS.)

SHANKS: Has anybody seen my trousers?

WICKSTEED: Who is this?

MRS. WICKSTEED: Probably a patient left over from surgery.

WICKSTEED: He is not my patient.

SHANKS: I'm not anybody's patient.

MRS. WICKSTEED: Then you've no business here. Get out.

SHANKS: You again. No. Please don't touch me. No. No. Keep off.

WICKSTEED: Odd. He seems to know you.

MRS. WICKSTEED: In my voluntary work I rub shoulders with all sorts. . . .

SHANKS: Don't let her touch me. You'll protect me won't you?

WICKSTEED: Against what?

SHANKS: Against her.

MRS. WICKSTEED: I don't want to touch you.

SHANKS: You did before.

MRS. WICKSTEED: Hold your tongue.

WICKSTEED: Before? Before what, Muriel?

MRS. WICKSTEED: I don't know. How am I supposed to know?

SHANKS: She's a monster.

WICKSTEED: She is not a monster. She is my wife.

SHANKS: She's sex mad.

MRS. WICKSTEED: Listen, I wear the corsets in this house, so shut your cake-hole, before I give you a bunch of fives.

WICKSTEED: Muriel. Is there something between you and this man?

MRS. WICKSTEED: Arthur. I am not friends if you say things like that. It's quite plainly a delusion.

SHANKS: A delusion? Is this a delusion?
    (*He shows him the Polaroid snaps.*)
    Or this? The camera cannot lie.

WICKSTEED: What wonderful pictures. Who is it?

SHANKS: Who? It's her.

WICKSTEED: Good God. So it is. Muriel, what have you got to say?

MRS. WICKSTEED: Damn. Damn. I am ruined.

WICKSTEED: Is this your clear conscience? Qu'est-ce que c'est que ça madame? Not to mention ça.

MRS. WICKSTEED: Silliness, silliness. That was all it was.

WICKSTEED: Is this your innocence?
    (*He plucks at* SHANKS' *shirt-tails.*)
    Or this?

SHANKS: Stop it.

WICKSTEED: So. Now it's my turn.

MRS. WICKSTEED: No. Arthur, please.

WICKSTEED: Don't touch me. Don't touch me. You're not fit to touch me.

MRS. WICKSTEED: It was a mistake.

WICKSTEED: And don't grovel. I can't abide a groveller. You see, I always thought no one else fancied her. I've always had this sneaking feeling that if I hadn't married her, no one else would. But (*he looks at the snaps*) my goodness me! It's *Forever Amber* all over again. Flower arrangements,

57

cake decorating. All those long suburban afternoons. . . . It was lovers, lovers from all walks of life, like you. How long has this been going on?

MRS. WICKSTEED: This afternoon. Ten minutes. That's all.

WICKSTEED: I don't believe it. I believe it's been going on for years. Sex isn't something that happens overnight, you know.

MRS. WICKSTEED: You're wrong, so wrong.

WICKSTEED: Go to your room. Pack one or two things, just in case. You may have to go to your mother's. (*To* SHANKS.) And you, get out.

SHANKS: I'd like to ex. . . .

WICKSTEED: Get out.

MRS. WICKSTEED (*returning*): Arthur.

WICKSTEED: Yes.

MRS. WICKSTEED: Am I to be turned out of my own house?

WICKSTEED: I was.

MRS. WICKSTEED: Can't we forgive and forget? We can live on our memories.

WICKSTEED: I have no memories, only scars.

MRS. WICKSTEED: Arthur, please.

WICKSTEED: No, Muriel.

(*She exits.*)

WICKSTEED: The eyes, cool but kindly, looked back unflinchingly from the glass. There was pain in those eyes, a hint perhaps of some secret sorrow. He ran his lean brown fingers through his thinning hair and sighed. And yet, at the corner of his firm, yet sensitive mouth, there hovered the merest suspicion of a smile. "I'm still in the game" he thought. (*Exits.*)

(*Enter* SHANKS.)

MRS. SWABB: I see you're still in your underpants. And the same pair too. Have you never heard of the dictum: undies worn twice are not quite nice?

SHANKS: No. (*Exits.*)

MRS. SWABB: And they talk of comprehensive education.

(*Enter* PURDUE.)

PURDUE: That is the dirtiest gas oven I've ever put my head in.

MRS. SWABB: It's not gas, it's electric. (*Exits.*)

(FELICITY *and* DENNIS *enter.*)

DENNIS: Felicity.

FELICITY: I gave her the slip. I had to see you again.

DENNIS: Yes. I feel the same way. Except. . . .

FELICITY: Except what?

DENNIS: Could you love me if I wasn't going to die?

FELICITY: But you are.

DENNIS: I mean we all die sooner or later. So say it was later rather than sooner.

FELICITY: How much later?

DENNIS: Roundabout the time you're supposed to die, three score years and ten.

FELICITY: How much is that?

DENNIS: Seventy.

FELICITY: Another fifty years. No, my love, we must resign ourselves, there is no hope.

DENNIS: No. I don't think there is.

SHANKS: At last.

MRS. SWABB: Oh no. Not again.

(SHANKS *approaches* FELICITY.)

SHANKS: I had rather an unpleasant experience earlier, so you'll forgive me if I'm cautious.

FELICITY: How do you do.

SHANKS: I thought I must be losing my touch. But no. One look at you and I realize, those could never be real.

(MRS. SWABB, DR. *and* MRS. WICKSTEED, DENNIS, FELICITY, CANON THROBBING *and* CONNIE *have come on to the stage and are watching, fascinated.*)

SHANKS: The line so crisp, the silhouette so pert. If that's not our product I'll go back to chicken farming.

(*He touches* FELICITY'S *breast and she slaps his face.*)

MRS. WICKSTEED: I second that. (*Fetches him another.*)

SHANKS: I can't understand it. On the training course they teach you to tell blindfold.

WICKSTEED: What are you doing here, anyway?

SHANKS: I'm looking for my client.

(FELICITY *slaps him again.*)

DENNIS: Without your trousers?

59

THROBBING: Is he a commercial traveller?

(CONNIE *slaps* THROBBING.)

SHANKS: In a sense.

DENNIS: If he's a commercial traveller, he must often be without his trousers.

(WICKSTEED *slaps* DENNIS.)

MRS. WICKSTEED: Arthur!

THROBBING: What do you travel in?

(CONNIE *slaps* THROBBING, MRS. WICKSTEED *slaps* WICKSTEED, SHANKS *slaps* DENNIS, WICKSTEED *slaps* MRS. WICKSTEED *as* LADY RUMPERS *enters.*)

MRS. SWABB: Delia, Lady Rumpers.

LADY RUMPERS: Out of my way, you pert slut. Is this what we were promised when we emerged from the Dark Ages? Is this Civilization? I'm only thankful Kenneth Clark isn't here to see it.

MRS. SWABB: I'm not actually sure he isn't.

LADY RUMPERS (*to* SHANKS): You.

SHANKS: Good evening.

LADY RUMPERS: Good evening. What has happened to your trousers?

SHANKS: I don't know.

LADY RUMPERS: Well you'd better find them. If I'd wanted to see people running about in their shirt-tails I should have stayed in Addis Ababa.

CONNIE: Good evening.

LADY RUMPERS: Good evening.

THROBBING: Good evening.

LADY RUMPERS: Good evening. Why should your face be familiar? Have you ever been called to serve the Lord in heathen parts?

THROBBING: Well, I was for a short time a curate in Leeds.

MRS. WICKSTEED: Good evening.

WICKSTEED: Good evening.

LADY RUMPERS: All in all I can say quite confidently I have seen nothing like this even in the cesspots of Mespot. And Felicity, leave that dismal boy alone.

WICKSTEED: Hear, hear.

LADY RUMPERS: Shut up. Do you hear?

FELICITY: No. I won't. I love Dennis.

DENNIS: We want to get married.

LADY RUMPERS: Love, Madam. I do not want to hear that word. You talk of love with a body like yours. Time enough to fall back on love when the bloom begins to fade. I didn't slave away bringing you up in a temperature of 115 in the shade for you to talk of love as soon as my back is turned.

WICKSTEED: I quite agree.

LADY RUMPERS: Shut up.

MRS. WICKSTEED: Hear, hear.

LADY RUMPERS: You too. The word marriage has been mentioned. It is out of the question. Felicity is far too young for a start. . . .

FELICITY: But Mother.

LADY RUMPERS: And the young man.

WICKSTEED: Keith.

MRS. WICKSTEED: Dennis.

LADY RUMPERS: . . . far too ugly.

WICKSTEED: True. A boy like that proposing marriage to a girl the strap of whose bra he is not worthy to undo.

LADY RUMPERS: Don't touch her.

THROBBING: Could I say something?

LADY RUMPERS: ⎫
CONNIE: ⎬No.

MRS. WICKSTEED: May a mother have a voice?

LADY RUMPERS: ⎫
WICKSTEED: ⎬No.

LADY RUMPERS: A girl like Felicity and a shrivelled thing like him. Think of the stock. Why you wouldn't do it to a hyacinth.

MRS. WICKSTEED: Hyacinths don't fall in love.

WICKSTEED: If you ask me, he wants a kick up the arse.

LADY RUMPERS: Come, Felicity. It's time we were going. When I hear the word arse I know the way the wind is blowing.

MRS. WICKSTEED: Lady Rumpers. Arthur. One moment. May a mother speak? Fair dos. We're all of us pretty well headed for the sere and yellow. Its times hurrying footsteps all

61

round these days, isn't it? Now Dennis, he's not a glamour puss. Never will be. Even though he is the fruit of our loins. Partly our fault. Funny boy. Difficult to love. Never liked touching him very much and quite frankly it makes a difference. Touching, looking, loving . . . without it which one of us would thrive? Look at your girl, Felicity. Stroked and cherished all her life. Lovely girl.

LADY RUMPERS: Lovely girl.

WICKSTEED: Lovely girl.

MRS. WICKSTEED: But that's because she's been worn next to the heart. Result: she blooms. Dennis, shoved away at the back of the drawer, result: drab, boring, spotty, nobody wants him.

CONNIE: But that's me too.

MRS. WICKSTEED: But I say this: love him, as your girl seems unaccountably to love him, and he'll blossom.

MRS. SWABB: I think he's looking better already.

LADY RUMPERS: No, never. It's quite right you should be kind to him. You are his mother. I am under no such handicap.

CONNIE: Please.

LADY RUMPERS: No.

MRS. SWABB: Please.

LADY RUMPERS: No.

DENNIS: Please.

LADY RUMPERS: No.

FELICITY: Please.

LADY RUMPERS: No. My daughter. . . .

WICKSTEED: Oh, stuff your daughter.

MRS. SWABB (*indicating* DENNIS): He already has.

LADY RUMPERS: What?

(LADY RUMPERS *gives a great cry and swoons.*)

MRS. SWABB: Did I strike a wrong note?

WICKSTEED: Excuse me, I'm a doctor.

MRS. WICKSTEED: We know you're a doctor.

WICKSTEED: She has fainted.

MRS. WICKSTEED: Dennis, is this true?

MRS. SWABB: Quite true. Between 15.10 and 15.25 this afternoon they carried out the docking procedure.

WICKSTEED: You mean, you and her, her and you?

DENNIS: Yes.

THROBBING: What was it like?

LADY RUMPERS: After all my precautions. Gone. Tossed away on him.

FELICITY: No. It was love.

LADY RUMPERS: Love. You don't understand. No one understands. The shame. The waste. My own shameful story all over again.

MRS. WICKSTEED: Oh crumbs!

LADY RUMPERS: Many years ago, when I was not much older than Felicity is now, I had just arrived in the colonies . . . I . . . you have to know this Felicity. I should have told you before. I had just arrived in the colonies when I found I was P-R-E-G-N-A-N-T.

THROBBING: PRAGNANT?

MRS. WICKSTEED: Pegnat.

LADY RUMPERS: PREGNANT. I was not married at the time.

MRS. WICKSTEED: What about General Rumpers?

LADY RUMPERS: Tiger and I met soon afterwards. He loved me . . . I . . . respected him. We married. He was a gentleman but shy. He only went into the Army in order to put his moustache to good purpose. He was glad of a child for his life too had its secrets: a passing-out party at Sandhurst had left him forever incapable of having children. He threw the blanket of his name over Felicity and together we achieved respectability. Call me fool, call me slut, call me anything you like. But I vowed at that time that the same thing should never happen to Felicity. And now it has. My poor child. Oh Felicity, Felicity.

WICKSTEED: And where is he now, her real father?

LADY RUMPERS: Do you think I have not asked myself that question? Lying under mosquito nets in Government House do you think that question has not hammered itself into my brain?

WICKSTEED: Have you any clues?

LADY RUMPERS: One and one only. He was a doctor. Yes. That is why I despise your profession.

MRS. WICKSTEED: His name. Do you not know that?

LADY RUMPERS: No. I suppose that shocks you.

MRS. WICKSTEED: Nothing could shock me any more.

LADY RUMPERS: Picture the scene. Liverpool. The blitz at its height. I am bound for the Far East. Our convoy is assembled ready to go down the Mersey on the morning tide. Suddenly I am told I cannot sail.

WICKSTEED: Yes?

LADY RUMPERS: No. I had no vaccination certificate. The blackout. An air-raid in progress. The docks ablaze. I set off alone to find a doctor. Buildings crashing all round me. Crash, crash, crash. Bombs raining down on the street. Boom, boom, boom. I see a brass plate. The surgery in darkness. The doctor under the table. He writes me a certificate. I am grateful. Think how grateful I was. We talk.

THROBBING: Yes, yes, go on.

LADY RUMPERS: Two voices in the darkness of the surgery as the storm rages outside. His hand steals into mine. . . .

THROBBING: Yes, then what did he do? . . .

LADY RUMPERS: We cling to each other as the bombs fell.

THROBBING: Yes?

LADY RUMPERS: I need not tell you the rest.

THROBBING: They always miss out the best bits.

LADY RUMPERS: The All Clear sounds as I stumble back on board. Came the dawn we slipped out of the Mersey and headed for the open sea. Do you know the Atlantic at all?

MRS. WICKSTEED: No.

LADY RUMPERS: It is very rough. I thought I was sea sick. Only when we docked did I realize I had a bun in the club.

MRS. WICKSTEED: Tragic.

WICKSTEED: Wonderful.

LADY RUMPERS: I blame the War.

WICKSTEED: Ah the War, that was a strange and wonderful time.
        Oh Mavis and Audrey and Lilian and Jean
        Patricia and Pauline and NAAFI Christine
        Maureen and Myrtle I had you and more
        In God's gift to the lecher the Second World War.

MRS. SWABB: In shelters and bunkers on Nissen hut floors,
They wrestled with webbing and cellular drawers.
From pillbox on headland they scoured the seas
While pinching our bottoms and stroking our
knees.

LADY RUMPERS: Echoes of music drift into the night.
Never in peace will it all seem so right.

WICKSTEED: Oh Lost Generation where are you now?
I still see Lemira, Yvonne's in Slough.
Mothers like you, with girls in their twenties.
Fathers like me: we all share such memories.

LADY RUMPERS: One mad magenta moment and I have paid for
it all my life. Felicity ruined.

MRS. SWABB: We don't know she is, do we? One swallow doesn't
make a summer.

FELICITY: Never mind, Mummy. After all he wants to marry me.

LADY RUMPERS: Yes. Go Felicity. Be happy.

FELICITY: Happy. Oh Mummy, if you only knew.

WICKSTEED: Such a waste.

MRS. WICKSTEED: At least somebody's happy.

WICKSTEED: Is she happy?

MRS. SWABB: She looks happy to me. But then I'm a
behaviourist.

MRS. WICKSTEED: You're a busybody.

MRS. SWABB: And I can make her happier still.

FELICITY: Nobody can make me happier.

MRS. SWABB: I can. I want to explain about Dennis.

DENNIS: No, Mrs. Swabb, no.

FELICITY: Such a short time we have together.

MRS. SWABB: But it isn't.

FELICITY: It's three months.

MRS. SWABB: No.

FELICITY: No?

DENNIS: No.

FELICITY: Longer?

MRS. SWABB: Yes.

DENNIS: No.

FELICITY: Much longer?

MRS. SWABB: Much, much longer.

FELICITY: You mean . . . he's not going to die at all?

MRS. SWABB: Strong as a horse.

DENNIS: } Oh, no.
FELICITY:

MRS. SWABB: It's all in the mind.

WICKSTEED: This doctor in Liverpool, I'm interested. What did he look like?

LADY RUMPERS: As I say there was a black-out. I saw his face only in the fitful light of a post-coital Craven A. He was small, but perfectly proportioned. In some respects more so. I don't suppose I shall ever find him.

MRS. SWABB: Who knows. One day the doorbell will go and he will walk back into her life.

(*Bell.*)

THROBBING: Isn't that the doorbell?

WICKSTEED: Don't lets jump to conclusions. It could be the man next door taking his first tentative steps on the xylophone.

MRS. SWABB: Sir Percy Shorter.

SIR PERCY: I wish to speak to your daughter.

LADY RUMPERS: My daughter has been spoken to by at least four people this afternoon, one of whom has proposed marriage. Naturally, she is exhausted.

SIR PERCY: I wish to take down her evidence.

MRS. WICKSTEED: You've taken down quite enough this afternoon.

SIR PERCY: LIES, LIES.

LADY RUMPERS: What sort of evidence?

SIR PERCY: She has this very afternoon been assaulted.

MRS. WICKSTEED: Haven't we all.

LADY RUMPERS: Suffice it to say that my daughter is to marry the person who assaulted her.

SIR PERCY: But he is married already. To this lady. (*Indicating* MRS. WICKSTEED.)

LADY RUMPERS: Indeed. She has been masquerading as his mother. These are new depths.

WICKSTEED: Understandably Sir Percy is a little confused.

SIR PERCY: Little!

WICKSTEED: He is over-excited. You are over-excited.

SIR PERCY: That is not true. I was never more calm in my life. I am the only person here telling the truth. Unclean, unclean. I'll break you. Under cover of a medical examination this man assaulted your daughter.

LADY RUMPERS: You? My daughter appears to have been assaulted by the whole family.

MRS. WICKSTEED: No. Not me.

WICKSTEED: No. Not you. You confined yourself to our friend in the shirt-tails. You're the prey of any tom-cat that knocks at the door.

SIR PERCY (*to* WICKSTEED): You can talk.

MRS. WICKSTEED (*to* SIR PERCY): You can talk.

SHANKS (*to* MRS. WICKSTEED): You can talk.

THROBBING: I seem to be the only one with nothing to be ashamed of.

LADY RUMPERS: Now I remember you. You are the Beast of the 10.26. Just because you're a clergyman you think you can look up girls' legs.

CONNIE: Is this true?

THROBBING: One has to look somewhere.

CONNIE: Harold! Don't touch me.

FELICITY: Don't touch me. Don't touch me.

DENNIS: Penelope.

FELICITY: FELICITY. I despise you. You lied to me.

DENNIS: Not really.

FELICITY: I thought it was only going to be for three months.

DENNIS: But you said you loved me.

FELICITY: All your faults . . . the stuff you put on your hair, your awful trousers, your terrible terrible feet. For three months yes, I could swallow it all, string vests, everything. But not for *life*.

DENNIS: What if I promised to commit suicide at the end of three months?

FELICITY: It's very nice of you, but it wouldn't be the same. Don't touch me.

MRS. WICKSTEED: Arthur.

WICKSTEED: Don't touch me.

FELICITY (*to* DENNIS): Don't touch me.

WICKSTEED (*to* SIR PERCY): Don't touch me.

CONNIE (*to* THROBBING): Don't touch me.

SIR PERCY: All in all, I can say quite confidently that I've seen nothing like this since I was a locum in Liverpool.

(*All come on slowly, and stand in a great circle round* SIR PERCY.)

MRS. SWABB: And now, suddenly the air is black with the wings of chickens coming home to roost.

WICKSTEED: You did say Liverpool?

SIR PERCY: Liverpool.

LADY RUMPERS: Liverpool?

MRS. WICKSTEED: Liverpool.

MRS. SWABB: Liverpool.

SIR PERCY: Yes, Liverpool. What of it. I did a locum there. In the War.

WICKSTEED: Yes, of course, the War.

LADY RUMPERS: That would be the Second War, the one to make the world safe for democracy?

SIR PERCY: That was how it was advertised.

WICKSTEED: When the enemy was always listening, and cigarettes were two a penny. (*He lights a cigarette lighter.*)

MRS. SWABB: Put that light out.

(*Darkness, the sounds of an air-raid.*)

LADY RUMPERS: That's him! That's him!

SIR PERCY: Who?

LADY RUMPERS: My seducer.

SIR PERCY: Are you all mad?

WICKSTEED: Liverpool. The War. The docks. Yes?

SIR PERCY: No.

WICKSTEED: Buildings crashing down. Whole streets ablaze. Yes?

SIR PERCY: No. No.

WICKSTEED: A doctor's surgery. Yes?

SIR PERCY: I don't remember.

WICKSTEED: Your surgery.

SIR PERCY: No.

WICKSTEED: And then, a knock comes at the door. It is a patient. A woman.

SIR PERCY: It could have been anybody.

WICKSTEED: But it wasn't anybody.

SIR PERCY: It was nobody.

LADY RUMPERS: Nobody! It was me!

    (*Lights up.*)

SIR PERCY: You!

LADY RUMPERS: Don't you remember how we clung to each other in the darkness of the surgery?

THROBBING: Yes. Yes. Tell it like it is.

SIR PERCY: No.

LADY RUMPERS: And then you took me.

THROBBING: Yee-ow.

SIR PERCY: I took *you*? You took *me*. Your Land Army breeches came down with a fluency born of long practice.

LADY RUMPERS: It is immaterial.

THROBBING: Could we go back over that bit in more detail?

SIR PERCY: No.

THROBBING: They've missed it out again.

LADY RUMPERS: There was a child. She lived and found powerful friends. She is living now. She is a lady and very beautiful.

DENNIS: And I love her.

    (FELICITY *weeps*.)

SIR PERCY: What's the matter with her.

WICKSTEED: It must be something of a shock to find she's got you for a father.

SIR PERCY: Father? Me? Bless her. To think, all these years denied the chance of lavishing on her fatherly affections. Those little services of love which are a father's right. Stroke her hair, wipe away her tears, bath her.

LADY RUMPERS: Bath her?

SIR PERCY: Well, perhaps no. But help her choose her dresses, rub on her suntan lotion . . . those one hundred and one things only a father can do. You can see she needs a father's hand.

WICKSTEED: Not down her blouse.

LADY RUMPERS: I see you haven't changed. No word of regret.

SIR PERCY: The incident had vanished from my mind.

LADY RUMPERS: You funny little man.

SIR PERCY: Don't say that.

LADY RUMPERS: Rumpers was a little man too. He made no
    secret of his height. Strange, I've been looking for you all
    my life and now I've found you I don't know what to do
    with you.
SIR PERCY: You've got nothing to do with me.
LADY RUMPERS: You don't even seem sorry.
SIR PERCY: Why should I be sorry? I didn't know there was a
    child.
WICKSTEED: And are you in the habit of seducing every patient
    who comes into your surgery?
SIR PERCY: It was the War.
WICKSTEED: And Lady Rumpers was your patient?
SIR PERCY: No.
LADY RUMPERS: You were the doctor, I was the patient and
    Felicity was the outcome. (*Exits.*)
WICKSTEED: Tut, tut, tut. Hard lines, Perce.
SIR PERCY: Don't call me Perce. I am Sir Percy Shorter,
    President of the BMA.
WICKSTEED: Not for much longer.
SIR PERCY: You wouldn't dare.
WICKSTEED: I would. Unprofessional conduct. Interfering with
    patients. A list of charges as long as your arm, no, my arm.
    And the chief witness your own illegitimate daughter. I
    think it's sleeping dogs time, Percy. Otherwise one word and
    it's curtains, finito.
SIR PERCY: It's not fair. Why is it always me?
WICKSTEED: How extraordinary! so even you, Percy are human.
    Just like all the rest of us, the world over. Each one of us
    walking the world because someone somewhere happened to
    bring their body and lay it against another body. Everyone.
    Every person you see in the street, read about in the
    newspaper. All the names in the births column. All the
    names in the deaths column. Chinese swimming rivers with
    guns in their mouths, the Ryder Cup team. The Pope on
    his balcony. Everybody. Everywhere. All the time.
MRS. SWABB (*bowing deeply*): Sir Percy. Could I crave a boon?
SIR PERCY: She's mad too. They're all in the plot.
MRS. SWABB: Examine Dennis. Tell her he's dying. Pretend.

SIR PERCY: Pretend? Tell her, who? Why?

MRS. SWABB: Felicity.

SIR PERCY: My daughter? Pretend? I couldn't pretend that. I couldn't. You don't know what you're asking. My position. Jeopardizing my professional integrity.

MRS. SWABB: You haven't got any. Not now.

SIR PERCY: Nobody knows that.

MRS. SWABB: They could always find out.

SIR PERCY: LIES. LIES. Blackmail. It's a PLOT. I WILL NEVER DO IT. NEVER NEVER NEVER. Where is he?

MRS. SWABB: Follow me, Sir Percy. I will conduct you thither.

(*Enter* CONNIE *and* FELICITY *each looking at themselves.*)

CONNIE: It used to be so flat.

FELICITY: It used to be so flat.

CONNIE: Can you tell?

FELICITY: You can tell.

(SHANKS, *in Purdue's trousers comes upon* CONNIE *still trying to adjust her bust.*)

SHANKS: Something tells me you're the person we're looking for. Miss Wicksteed?

CONNIE: Yes.

SHANKS: Allow me. There. Striking without being indiscreet. Full but not vulgar. What a day. Would you like to take a walk?

CONNIE: In the street? Won't people stare?

SHANKS: At a striking woman. Yes. People will stare.

CONNIE: I shall need different clothes, a larger fit. My hair ought to be different. My whole style.

SHANKS: Come. The world is waiting.

(*Exit* SHANKS *and* CONNIE.)

(*Enter* SIR PERCY, *with* DENNIS *and* MRS. SWABB.)

SIR PERCY: There is no doubt about it. Brett's Palsy.

MRS. SWABB: Brett's Palsy. How terrible. How terrible, Felicity.

DENNIS: Don't overdo it.

SIR PERCY: In it's tertiary stage.

MRS. SWABB: Tertiary. That's good. Tertiary is good. Tertiary is very good.

DENNIS: How long have I got?

SIR PERCY: Do you really want me to tell you?

DENNIS: For the sake of my fiancée, yes.

FELICITY: Your former fiancée. I gave you back the ring.

SIR PERCY: In the circumstances a wise precaution. Your engagement would have been broken off anyway.

FELICITY: You mean. . . ?

SIR PERCY: I'm afraid so. Three months. Four at the outside.

FELICITY: You're sure?

MRS. SWABB: President of the BMA. Physician to the Queen, course he's sure. A man in his position can't afford to make mistakes, can you.

SIR PERCY: No.

FELICITY: Oh Dennis. Forgive me.

DENNIS: So I do have Brett's Palsy after all. I knew I had Brett's Palsy. I always said I had Brett's Palsy. Felicity, how could you ever have doubted I had Brett's Palsy. Time is short. We must be married this minute. (*They exit.*)

MRS. SWABB: That was very sporting of you, Sir Percy.

SIR PERCY: Not difficult. Really rather sad.

MRS. SWABB: Sad? Why?

SIR PERCY: He has three months to live. He thought he had Brett's Palsy. He has got Brett's Palsy. As paranoids sometimes have enemies, so hypochondriacs sometimes have diseases. It isn't always in the mind.

MRS. SWABB: But he's so happy.

SIR PERCY: So what are you weeping about. He's happy. He's got his lady love. She's happy. She thinks he's going to die. He is going to die. Everybody's happy. Except me.

MRS. SWABB: Well we're into injury time now.

There's no time to make a rhyme up.

Just the wedding and the line up.

MRS. WICKSTEED: Dear Dennis, I hope he's making the right decision.

WICKSTEED: What does it matter? He's in love.

MRS. WICKSTEED: And we're back where we started.

WICKSTEED: I say love. That great conglomerate. Affection and attraction, envy and desire. All marketed under the same label. A father's love, a daughter's love, love of wives for

72

husbands and mothers for children. Its love all right. But which department . . . the headquarters in the heart or the depot between the legs?

MRS. WICKSTEED: Do try not to be vulgar, Arthur, or we shall never get on.

WICKSTEED: Only time will tell.

MRS. SWABB: Delia, Lady Rumpers.

LADY RUMPERS: From youth and from desiring
From love and passion free
Old with too much regretting
My future's plain to see.
A small hotel in Eastbourne
A nightly game of whist.
An old colonial lady
Who'll die and not be missed.

SIR PERCY: But Delia I too am lonely
For lonely are the brave
Come. Why do we not go together,
In step towards the grave?

MRS. SWABB: So as the shadows lengthen
Across the lawns of life
They walk into the sunset . . .
Sir Percy and his wife.

(CONNIE *sweeps on, transformed, with* SHANKS.)
These flashing legs
This smile so regal.
I know that face.
Dame Anna Neagle!

CONNIE: No, no. You fool. It's me, it's me.
Got up like an awful tart,
But ready now to pay to Life
The debt I owe to Art.
My new fiancée, Denzil here,
Is keen on heavy petting
He wants to go too far with me
And by God I'm going to let him.

THROBBING (*to* CONNIE): Your future hopes, your married bliss
On firm foundations rest.

Who knows, one day, I just might be.
A guest upon that breast.
My life I squandered waiting
Then let my chance go by.
One day we'll meet in Heaven.
That Matlock in the sky.

MRS. SWABB: That's a refreshing change. The first time this
evening everyone has had their trousers on.

(*Enter* PURDUE *without trousers.*)

I might have known. Where are your trousers?

PURDUE: I gave them to him. You don't need trousers
where I'm going. I've just taken fifty sleeping pills.
The pink ones.

WICKSTEED: Those aren't sleeping pills. They're laxatives.

MRS. SWABB: He's right. You don't need trousers where he's
going.

(THROBBING *presides over wedding of* DENNIS *and* FELICITY.)

DENNIS: Yes, I take this woman.

    For my lawful wedded wife.

FELICITY: To honour, love and cherish.

    The remainder of his life.

DENNIS: It will be longer than she thinks.

MRS. SWABB: And shorter than he knows.

FELICITY: My breast is filled with happiness.

CONNIE: And mine with cellulose.

(*All dance.*)

MRS. SWABB: The body's an empty vessel,

    The flesh an awful cheat,
    The world is just an abattoir,
    For our rotting lumps of meat.
    So if you get your heart's desire,
    Your longings come to pass,
    Remember in each other's beds
    It isn't going to last.
    The smoothest cheek will wrinkle
    The proudest breast will fall.
    Some sooner go, some later
    But death will claim us all.

WICKSTEED: No, no, no. Well, yes . . . but. . . .

MRS. WICKSTEED: But what?

WICKSTEED: But on those last afternoons in the bed by the door.
On the Clement Attlee Ward,
When you mourn the loss of energy
Even Lucozade cannot replace
And Sister Tudor thinks you may go any time
Do you think that you think
Of the things that you did
Or the things that you didn't do?
The promise broken, the meeting you missed,
The word not spoken, the cheek not kissed.
Lust was it or love? Was it false or true?
Who cares now?
Dying you'll grieve for what you didn't do.
The young are not the innocent, the old are not the
    wise,
Unless you've proved it for yourselves,
Morality is lies.
So this is my prescription: grab any chance you get
Because if you take it or you leave it,
You end up with regret.

    (*All go, leaving him.*)

    Put it this way.

A VOICE: Arthur.

WICKSTEED: Whatever right or wrong is
He whose lust lasts, lasts longest.

    (*He dances alone in the spotlight until he can dance no more.*)

CURTAIN